Fre

M000218410

This book is a meditation on the role of psychoanalysis within Latin literary studies. Neither a skeptic nor a true believer, Oliensis adopts a pragmatic approach to her subject, emphasizing what psychoanalytic theory has to contribute to interpretation. Drawing especially on Freud's work on dreams and slips, she spotlights textual phenomena that cannot be securely anchored in any intention or psyche but that nevertheless, or for that very reason, seem fraught with meaning; the "textual unconscious" is her name for the indefinite place from which these phenomena erupt, or which they retroactively constitute, as a kind of "unconsciousness-effect." The discussion is organized around three key topics in psychoanalysis – mourning, motherhood, and the origins of sexual difference – and takes the poetry of Catullus, Virgil, and Ovid as its point of reference. A brief afterword considers Freud's own witting and unwitting engagement with the idea of Rome.

ELLEN OLIENSIS is Professor of Classics at the University of California, Berkeley. She is the author of *Horace and the Rhetoric of Authority* (1998) as well as assorted essays on Latin literature.

# ROMAN LITERATURE
# AND ITS CONTEXTS

## Freud's Rome

# ROMAN LITERATURE
# AND ITS CONTEXTS

*Series editors*
Denis Feeney and Stephen Hinds

This series promotes approaches to Roman literature which are open to dialogue with current work in other areas of the classics, and in the humanities at large. The pursuit of contacts with cognate fields such as social history, anthropology, history of thought, linguistics and literary theory is in the best traditions of classical scholarship: the study of Roman literature, no less than Greek, has much to gain from engaging with these other contexts and intellectual traditions. The series offers a forum in which readers of Latin texts can sharpen their readings by placing them in broader and better-defined contexts, and in which other classicists and humanists can explore the general or particular implications of their work for readers of Latin texts. The books all constitute original and innovative research and are envisaged as suggestive essays whose aim is to stimulate debate.

# Freud's Rome

## Psychoanalysis and Latin Poetry

### Ellen Oliensis

*Professor of Classics,*
*University of California,*
*Berkeley*

CAMBRIDGE UNIVERSITY PRESS
Cambridge, New York, Melbourne, Madrid, Cape Town, Singapore,
São Paulo, Delhi, Dubai, Tokyo

Cambridge University Press
The Edinburgh Building, Cambridge CB2 8RU, UK

Published in the United States of America by Cambridge University Press, New York

www.cambridge.org
Information on this title: www.cambridge.org/9780521609104

First published 2009

Printed in the United Kingdom at the University Press, Cambridge

*A catalogue record for this publication is available from the British Library*

ISBN 978-0-521-84661-5 Hardback
ISBN 978-0-521-60910-4 Paperback

# Contents

# Acknowledgments

I never meant to write this book; I'm not sure exactly what happened. I was diverted from another project (my "official" project) by the need to produce a different sort of paper for a conference on "The Vergilian Century," held at the University of Pennsylvania in fall 2000. So I owe a special debt to Joe Farrell for designing the conference and including me in it, and to the other participants for their generous reception of my inchoate Freudian meditations; these subsequently appeared in *Vergilius* 47 (2001) and are reworked here in chapter 2. I developed the reading of Ovid's Scylla in chapter 3 in honor of Don Fowler, for a Memorial Lecture presented under the auspices of Jesus College Oxford in 2003; my thanks to Armand D'Angour for his exemplary hospitality on that occasion. I am grateful to have had the chance to try out various parts of the argument on audiences at Princeton University, Rice University, Stanford University, the University of Georgia, the USC/UCLA Latin seminar, and the UC Berkeley Townsend Center. As I neared the end, Norbert Lain talked me through some textual problems in Catullus, Seth Schein provided thoughtful comments on chapter 2, and Leslie Kurke read through and commented on the whole. The book's journey through the production process was eased by the ministrations of my research assistants, Chris Churchill and Jared Hudson, and, on the other side of the Atlantic, by the capable team at the Press. I could never have completed the project without the support of my department and university, the American Council of Learned Societies, the Loeb Classical Library Foundation, and the Townsend Center at UC Berkeley.

Finally, I need to thank all those who variously fostered this project during the long years when it was slowly slowly creeping toward the light of day, especially Alessandro Barchiesi, Joe Farrell, Nancy Felson, Mark Griffith, Tom Habinek, Leslie Kurke, Tony Long, Rebecca Shoptaw, and Liz Young. Special thanks to Janet Adelman, my mentor at the Townsend Center, for helping me understand what I was trying to accomplish; to John Shoptaw, for keeping me company through countless drafts; and to Stephen Hinds and Denis Feeney, for their patience, support, and invaluable editorial feedback.

I don't usually bother with the "all errors remaining" clause, but in this case I think I really ought to invoke it; so please consider it invoked.

Unless otherwise noted, I follow R. A. B. Mynors' Oxford text for Catullus and Virgil, and R. J. Tarrant's for Ovid's *Metamorphoses*.

# Introduction: Psychoanalysis
# and Latin poetry

## Why psychoanalysis?

This book is a self-conscious exercise in practical psychoanalysis, what might be called psychotextual criticism. It takes as its focus three poets who have been much on my mind over the last decade: Catullus, Virgil, and Ovid. Far from surveying psychoanalytic theory and critical practice, it constitutes my own idiosyncratic contribution, more Freudian than Lacanian and more literary than cultural, to the variegated tradition of psychoanalytically informed work within Classics.[1] The challenge I have set myself is to engage with psychoanalysis in all its seductive and rebarbative specificity while refraining from making myself too much at home in it – to embrace the discourse without defensive irony, but also without the fortifying passion of certainty. Accordingly, instead of mounting an all-out defense of psychoanalysis, I have chosen to confront theoretical issues as they present themselves in the course of reading. This book could also be described, then, as it were from the other side, as a trio of essays on Latin poetry interlaced with an ongoing assessment of the value of psychoanalysis for literary studies. Naturally, I believe that it does have value. The short answer to the question, "Why psychoanalysis?," an answer I hope subsequent chapters will substantiate, is: because I believe psychoanalysis still has something to

---

[1] Those seeking such an overview may turn to Wright (1998) and (for psychoanalysis within Classics, with a sample reading of *Antigone*) Griffith (2005). For a historicizing critique, engaged rather than dismissive, see duBois (1988). Good appreciations of Lacan in Janan (1994) 1–36; Porter and Buchan (2004a).

give to the practice of reading poetry; because I believe that it can provide news about poems, that it can make poems read differently – and this is always, for me, what matters the most.

Yet I need to acknowledge, here at the outset, that the question also carries, to my anxious ears at least, something of the urgency of a challenge or even a rebuke. Really now, in heaven's name, why would someone working with Latin poetry take up psychoanalysis of all things? For the truth is that psychoanalysis has always had a checkered reception within the discipline of Classics. On the one hand, this reception is part of the larger history (something of a tragicomedy, for those most directly involved on either side) of the contentious introduction of "foreign" ideas and practices, from New Criticism to New Historicism and beyond, into classical philology. Thirty years ago, no one would have dreamed that reputable classicists would one day be citing Foucault with Fraenkel or Lacan with Norden, but so it is; in our ever more comfortably eclectic world, the new hat and the old seem to go very well together. Certainly it seems safe to say, given the flood of psychoanalytic scholarship on the Latin side over the past decade, taking in Roman history, material culture, and philosophy as well as literature, that psychoanalysis has been absorbed into the mainstream of Roman studies. The best evidence for this absorption is that psychoanalysis can now be deployed not just as a master-discourse (as in Micaela Janan's programmatically Lacanian studies of Latin love poetry) but as one discourse in communication with others (as in Philip Hardie's recent work on Ovid, or Ellen O'Gorman's on the idea of Carthage).[2] Contemporary scholarship is dotted with the language of lack, desire, and repression, and terms of art such as the unconscious, the Real, and even *objet a* are beginning to sound (almost) familiar.

On the other hand, despite the warm welcome accorded psychoanalysis in so many quarters, the resistance continues almost as vigorous as ever. The problem is that psychoanalysis, unlike other approaches currently on offer, seems to depend on the critic's buying into the theory – not just thinking with the terms, but believing in the transhistorical

---

[2] Janan (1994), Janan (2001); Hardie (2002); O'Gorman (2004); more examples in Fredrick (2002) (the "Roman gaze"). A pair of Freudian examples: Mitchell-Boyask (1996) (on Virgil); Schiesaro (2003) (on Seneca). Absorption from the other direction: Galvagno (1995) (Lacan via Ovid).

validity of the stories from which they are culled. Thus interest in psychoanalysis has proceeded *pari passu* with the historicizing critique of Freudian theory.[3] In his 2002 handbook of theory for classicists, Thomas Schmitz puts the issue this way: "If Freud's theories really lack a scientific basis" – and Schmitz presumes they do – "any interpretation of literary texts or cultural phenomena inspired by these theories cannot claim any form of authority; concepts derived from psychoanalysis such as 'Oedipal' or 'phallic' would be mere metaphors without any validity."[4] "Repression, unconscious, desire, lack, other: with what stringency are these terms being used?," Denis Feeney likewise inquired in 1995. Used stringently, the terms carry, for most readers, too much baggage to carry conviction; used loosely, they devolve into figurality, leaving one "wondering," as Feeney puts it, "what the power of the model really is."[5]

The issue seems the more pressing for those who incline to Freud. How many scholars are prepared to stand up and be counted when (say) "penis envy" is on the agenda? Then again, how much meaning does the concept retain once domesticated as woman's envy of the prerogatives enjoyed by men in a patriarchal society? Lacanian theory is rendered more palatable by its structural and semiotic emphasis, to just the degree that the phallus as the primordial figure of signification (Lacan once playfully identified it with the bar in the Saussurean formula for the sign) is easier to take than the all-too-bodily penis. And yet the quasi-prophetic opacity of Lacan's writings, with their riddling pronouncements and elaborate mathematical formulae, provokes its own peculiarly intense forms of devotion and outrage and tends to produce an even harder division between believers and nonbelievers.

I raise the problem here at the outset, not because I hope to solve it to the satisfaction of anyone for whom it *is* a problem, but because I want to object to the way it is formulated. I don't agree that psychoanalytic reading is invalidated if its scientific basis is impugned – let me even say, for the sake of argument, now that its scientific basis has been exploded.

---

[3] Prominent examples include Vernant ([1967]1988) and Price (1990).

[4] Schmitz (2007) 197 (orig. publ. 2002 in German), in the course of an admirably forthright discussion of his reservations.

[5] Feeney (1995) 309, 310.

I don't believe that one must believe in the Oedipus complex, or any other complex, to find value in a psychoanalytic approach. What makes psychoanalysis psychoanalytic, in the end, is not any particular set of claims but a general orientation toward the unconscious and (in the largest sense) sexuality.[6] For a student of literature at least, sexuality is not something that compels or rebuffs belief. One may focus on incestuous desire or the construction of virility in a text without committing oneself to the proposition that it is sexuality that drives the psyche. But it is otherwise with the unconscious, and I will confess that there is a minimalist credo underlying this study, which could be articulated as follows: discourse regularly outruns the designs of the one deploying it; and this excess is structured and interpretable. In other words, I believe in the unconscious.

The admission will not, I hope, alienate too many of my readers, even those constitutionally hostile to psychoanalysis. Who does not believe as much? I take heart from the Freudian argument Feeney advances, no doubt quite self-consciously, immediately after registering his skepticism: "Whatever models we employ, we have to acknowledge that there is no use pretending that we are not employing them, and we also have to acknowledge that we will often be employing them unconsciously (they will be 'employing' *us*)."[7] One might argue that Feeney's use of "unconsciously" ought not to be assimilated to the psychoanalytic concept of the unconscious. Yet Freud's understanding of the effects of the unconscious was itself capacious, encompassing trivial social blunders as well as neurotic symptoms. Though gesturing toward the secret navel of the dream and the hidden springs of the joke, his endlessly proliferating local interpretations revel in the shallows, not the depths. It is thus entirely appropriate to speak of "Freudian slips" in ancient texts, whether feigned (as when Cicero refers to Clodius as Clodia's husband and then makes a show of correcting himself: "her brother I meant to say; I always make that mistake," *Cael.* 32) or staged as authentic (as when the hapless Lysidamus of Plautus' *Casina* keeps

---

[6] An oft-repeated claim; see, e.g., Lacan ([1953] 2006) 204. The most lucid and compelling account of psychoanalytic sexuality I have read is that of Laplanche (1976) 8–47.

[7] Feeney (1995) 310.

giving words to the desire he is laboring to conceal).[8] It may seem strange to invoke the unconscious here, given that Cicero and Lysidamus are both, albeit in different ways, "in the know." Yet the essential thing, for connoisseurs of the unconscious, is just the impression of alien interference, what Lacan calls "the sense of impediment": "In the dream, in the parapraxis, in the flash of wit – what is it that strikes one first? It is the sense of impediment to be found in all of them. Impediment, failure, split. In a spoken or written sentence something stumbles ... and it is there that [Freud] seeks the unconscious."[9] And this unconscious may be lurking just beneath the surface – or even in the next stanza.

Listening for the unconscious does not mean deauthorizing or discounting the artistry of the poetry. To the contrary, it means engaging strenuously and lovingly with its highly wrought texture.

## Whose unconscious?

Whose unconscious is it, then, that one is listening for?

Every answer presents its share of problems. (And the following review of these problems is not meant to suggest that this book will rise above them; to the contrary, it will remain enmeshed in them throughout.) Once upon a time, the normal default-answer was "the author's." But while many scholars are still willing to assign intentions to their authors, very few are prepared to set about uncovering their secret desires or buried memories; such psychobiographical speculations seem not just profitless but presumptuous, not to say hubristic. Another solution, one that has proven especially productive in recent years, is to focus on the "unconscious" of the culture at large. Most will agree that there are (linguistic, discursive, psychological, ideological) forces at work in textual production that exceed any individual author's control; no speech or writing could take place otherwise. Yet the idea of a "Roman unconscious" (vel sim.) only displaces the issue of the critic's superiority to the next level (the critic knows what the author unwittingly

---

[8] On the theoretical implications of Cicero's "Freudian slip," see Farrell (2005) 109–10; for the Plautine examples, Feldman (1962).

[9] Lacan ([1964] 1981) 25. I concede that this "sense of impediment" is susceptible to various interpretations; see, e.g., the robust polemic of Timpanaro (1976) (deploying textual criticism to refute Freud's analyses of slips).

communicates that the culture cannot fully express ... ).[10] At the other end of the communicative circuit, we are offered the reader's unconscious as the site of a transferential relation to the text, one that uncannily enacts and so produces the textual unconscious it purports to plumb.[11] Again, this solution strikes me as little more than a variation on the authorial unconscious, preferable from the standpoint of theoretical correctness perhaps, but without discernible consequences for reading. Surely the least fraught answer is the most traditional: the literary unconscious is a property of literary characters. As the example of Lysidamus suggests, the playwright's art readily extends to the creation of a character-unconscious; indeed, any characterized speaker, including the courtroom persona of a Cicero, may be so equipped. (The figure of self-correction, common to both examples, is a good index to this species of unconscious.) But even on the stage, of course, the issue is rarely this transparent. After all, characters are fabrications of language and their psychic depth is a mirage – a sort of verbal equivalent of the *trompe l'oeil* scenery they inhabit. And the instant we abandon the stage for nondramatic forms such as lyric and epic, the picture gets messier, as the boundaries around characters lose their rigidity, letting the unconscious seep out, as it were, into the surrounding text.

This seepage does not bother me, however. To the contrary, as I hope to demonstrate in the course of this book, psychoanalysis only gets more interesting as the outlines bleed. What I am listening for is an unconscious that tends to wander at will, taking up residence now with a character, now with the narrator, now with the impersonal narration, and sometimes flirting with an authorial or cultural address. Far from rejecting the answers outlined above, then, my solution, such as it is, is to embrace all of them. My shorthand term for this unanchored force is the "textual unconscious": "textual," because not (simply) personal, and also because it is in the very texture of the text, its slips, tics, strange emphases, and stray details, that one discovers it at work.[12] This may

---

[10] "Declamation offers insights into the Roman unconscious" (Gunderson (2003) 115); "elegiac discourse offers a privileged vantage point for observing the production of [a] split in the Roman subject" (Miller (2004) 26).

[11] Culler (1984).

[12] For the history of the term, see, conveniently, Mellard (2006) 13–17. My version overlaps with that of Riffaterre (1987) (though eschewing his emphasis on precision

sound like an evasion, and indeed it is. The textual unconscious is an enabling postulate, nothing more – though for my purposes, that is more than enough. I really don't mind bracketing unanswerable questions if that lets interpretation proceed. All I need to know for sure is that something is coming through, even if I can't pin down just where it is coming from.

An example or two may help explain why. My first is drawn from an essay by Emily Gowers on Horace *Satires* 1.7, a comic anecdote about a trial staged before the tyrannicide Brutus in Asia Minor; the dramatic setting of the satire thus falls in between the assassination of Julius Caesar and the defeat and suicide of the chief conspirators two years later. Gowers reads the satire (which dates from the subsequent decade) as an exploration of "the larger issues of the Revolution" ("tyranny, proscription, throat-cutting, silencing"), an exploration that both exploits and occludes Horace's own problematic involvement in that history, in particular "his participation on the wrong side" – Brutus' side – "at the battle of Philippi in 42 BCE." The evidence Gowers submits runs the gamut from the incontestable ("*Proscripti*, one can hardly avoid noticing, is the first word of Horace's poem") to what she acknowledges some will find "improbable": the recurrence of the word *lippus*, which she takes, along with conjunctions such as *Rupili pus* and *pila lippis*, as "a way of saying 'Philippi' … without quite saying it." Whose way? Though Gowers nowhere commits herself (and there is no reason she should), my sense is that, if pressed, she would claim that it is Horace's way: that the quasi-communication ("deliberately opaque," she suggests) is his. This would mean taking the poem as a knowing exercise in self-censorship, which it may well be; we will never know. But I for one would rather take these strange partial articulations as a kind of symptomatic stutter: an irruption of memory breaking through what Gowers at one point terms the "textual 'amnesia'" affecting Horace's writing of "the central trauma of his life."[13] Indeed, I would argue, it is precisely as a stutter, not as part of the overarching, explicit thematics of

and totalizability), but I am more in sympathy with Orlando (1978) (on the "return of the repressed" at the level of both form and content), and most in sympathy with Shoptaw (2000) (a capacious theorization, abundantly illustrated, of the interpretability of fragmentary and semi-intended textual phenonema).

[13] Gowers (2002); the citations are drawn from 146–52. In effect I am proposing to treat *Philippi* as what Shoptaw (2000) calls a "crypt word."

throat-cutting, that the effect takes on its full value as the just-audible index of an internalized censorship.

Is this then an authorial "slip," betraying the pressure of a history Horace seems intent on keeping under wraps? Have we found the author out? Possibly. Yet there are other solutions. Partisans of authorial control may prefer to argue that the irruption is designed to characterize the satiric persona as someone who can't (quite) keep his mouth shut, and/or his revolutionary times as inimical to the candor of Republican *libertas*. And intertextualists may choose to depersonalize the whole affair by locating "Philippi" in the discursive repertoire centered on Brutus, as if the very mention of Brutus sufficed to bring these deeply relevant phonemes into play. Yet what counts for me is less where the unconscious abides than what it does. The concept of the textual unconscious is meant to leave space for all possible locations while insisting on the interpretability of its effects. Moreover – and this is a crucial point – this interpretability is not just incidentally but essentially conditioned by the symptomatic incompleteness that attends it. The meaning dug up is never exhumed whole. Horace's satire does not mean "Philippi," or rather, it means it *and* does not. The goal of reading is not to replace a false surface with a true depth ("Philippi," after all, does reach the surface or Gowers would not be discussing it), but to bring into focus the energetic play of repression and circuitous expression that constitutes textuality.

In my second example the battle lines are drawn more sharply. Recently David Wray has taken issue with Paul Allen Miller's Lacanian reading of the Tibullan "dream text." The argument centers on the opening lines of Tibullus' first elegy and heats up with the fourth, almost untranslatable couplet (Tib. I.I.7–8):

> ipse seram teneras maturo tempore vites
> rusticus et facili grandia poma manu.

> Myself the farmer, I will sow the delicate vines when the time is ripe,
> and with easy hand the large fruits.

Miller's interpretation zeroes in on the strange adjective *facilis*: in what sense is a hand, and above all the hard-working hand of a farmer, appropriately described as "easy"?[14] The strangeness is compounded

---

[14] Miller (2004) 115–16.

by the "double displacement" produced by the illogical adjectives *maturo* and *grandia*, both denoting ripeness, hence redolent not of planting but of the harvest. The result, Miller argues, is an extraordinary condensation, "the presentation of the entire agricultural cycle ... in a single couplet."[15] The hand is "easy," one might say, because the farmer's labor, in this dreamy wish fulfillment, has been magically elided, along with the potentially treacherous months between sowing and reaping: the gratification is instantaneous. Yet as Miller stresses, in the Tibullan dream "the contradictory nature of our desires is represented but not transcended"; the dream is only a dream, a fragile bulwark erected against the pressure of the Real.[16]

In his Freudian theory of interpretation, Francesco Orlando rejects the noncommunicative model of the dream in favor of the pointed intentionality of the joke, a form of discourse that means to be understood.[17] What Wray finds problematic in Miller's "dream text" is likewise the displacement of communicative intention that it entails. For Miller, Tibullan "incoherence" is "symptomatic of the changing realm of the Real in post-civil-war Rome." For Wray, it is symptomatic rather of the critic's failure to work hard enough at resolving apparent incoherence into "a discursively intelligible poetic utterance."[18] Wray's solution here is to demonstrate that *facilis* is not merely unproblematic but ideally suited to its Tibullan context, a veritable *mot juste*: "by a calque on the Greek [ποιεῖν = *facere* "to make"], the speaker is describing his own hand neither as deft and masterful, nor as performing its work with effortless ease, but rather as ποιητικός: 'makerly' and so 'poetic.'" Thus in place of Miller's fable of the traumatic Real, Wray finds in these lines "a statement of poetic program, an *ars poetica*," one he shows to be deeply and widely rooted in ancient poetry and poetics.[19]

The opposition that emerges is perfectly exemplary. On one side, a dreaming poet subject to the forces of History; on the other, a

---

[15] Miller (2004) 116, 117.  [16] Miller (2004) 129.

[17] E.g., Orlando (1978) 5–6, 162–3; this dichotomy is complicated in his subsequent discussion of literature's "figurality rate" (163–70), a sliding scale from communicative transparency to noncommunicative opacity.

[18] Miller (2004) 129; Wray (2003) 221, reiterated at 246. (Wray is responding, much more appreciatively than my streamlined account suggests, to an earlier article version of Miller's (2004) book chapter.)

[19] Wray (2003) 232.

craftsman-poet in full command of all the resources of his tradition. The alternatives may seem irreconcilable. And yet, while I find Wray's discussion persuasive, it does not impel me to jettison Miller's account of the poem. Wray begins his essay on "easy hands" with the witty pronouncement "Tibullus is not an easy poet," and the issue of ease (and "difficulty") is everywhere folded into the argument: the critic (Wray seems wryly to tell us) has to labor so hard to solve the difficulty of the poet's "ease"![20] The curious thing about Wray's solution, however, is that it requires reading *facilis*, not just as a calque on ποιητικός, but *only* as such a calque; the solution depends on subtracting out the ordinary sense of *facilis* ( = "easy, yielding," etc.).[21] It depends on this, because the ordinary sense cuts across the antithesis of self-conscious craft ("making") vs. unconscious inspiration ("dreaming") that is pivotal to Wray's argument. After all (as Wray is aware), what the poets of craft harp on is not the ease but the *difficulty* of their art – the painful necessity of long hours of study, revision, and pruning, followed by a prolonged period of ripening (nine years, according to Horace!); "ease" is for inspired hacks – or for dreamers. Thus if *facilis* names the "poetic" art, it is only by repressing the lack of "easiness" at its heart.[22] It is this dimension of repression that Wray neglects and Miller captures.

Still, I remain sympathetic to the philological impulse underlying Wray's critique. Though I admire Miller's reading of the symptomatic complexity of the Tibullan couplet, I am less interested in his overarching Lacanian–Jamesonian story about the Real of History. Certainly it is not by chance that my favorite moment (and chapter) in Miller's book is this his most Freudian. I am not sure why it is so, but it seems to be true that Lacanian readers, though attending to the symptomatic surface of the text, tend on the whole to move away from that surface toward the abstractions (desire, Woman, the Symbolic, the split subject, etc.) they find reflected in it. This is a hallowed mode of interpretation, one shaped

---

[20] Wray (2003) 217 (on the critic's "difficulty," 221, 227).

[21] Wray (2003) 234–5. The production of *facilis* "makerly" via the repression of *facilis* "easy" exemplifies the workings of the Riffaterrean "intertextual unconscious," whereby "literary signs point to the unconscious inasmuch as they repress a meaning in the process of conveying one" (Riffaterre (1987) 213–14).

[22] Here as elsewhere psychoanalysis converges with deconstruction, a reading practice programmatically attuned to the textual unconscious (and much engaged with Freud's writings); see, e.g., Derrida (1987).

by the pressure of a philosophical engagement with the world of ideas.[23] Yet my own inclinations always tip me back into the text, and this effectively means back toward Freud: not Freud the myth-maker, but Freud the perpetual interpreter and avid student of the mechanisms of textual production.[24] Thus while this book shows the impress of Lacanian theory, and Kleinian theory too, for that matter, the "Freud" of *Freud's Rome* is not just a synecdoche for psychoanalysis.[25]

## What lies ahead

This book comprises three chapters, each of which addresses a nodal topic of psychoanalysis – mourning, motherhood, sexual difference – by way of a pair of readings. These topics are meant to represent a range of psychoanalytic theory without pretending to exhaust the possibilities (and readers will notice some glaring omissions).[26] Chapter 1 explores the pressure of mourning in the song of Ovid's Orpheus and the long poems of Catullus; chapter 2 tracks the ambivalent implications of motherhood through Virgil's *Aeneid* and Ovid's Philomela episode; and chapter 3 hunts the phallus across the middle books of Ovid's *Metamorphoses* and back again into the long poems of Catullus. An afterword offers a quick tour of Rome's place in the Freudian imaginary.

Though I don't know how many of my readers will begin at the beginning and continue straight on to the end, the book is designed for linear reading. The overall trajectory of the argument is from the reasonably familiar to the unabashedly weird – and this applies both to the themes discussed and to the reading strategies deployed. Everyone

---

[23] For a rare counter-example of Lacanian hyperliteralism, see Buchan (2004).

[24] Though one could substitute here the Lacan of "The instance of the letter" and the seminars on Joyce, I don't find that Lacan's "return to Freud" makes much of a difference in this area (by contrast with, say, his interventions on narcissism, the phallus, etc.).

[25] Granted, viewed from another angle, Freud and Lacan look much the same. Yet though classicists have made forays into object-relations theory (e.g., Mathews (2002)), my emphasis on Freud and Lacan reflects the state of play in the field along with my own formalist tendencies.

[26] Most notably that quintessentially Freudian topic, the Oedipus complex, slighted here (though see chapter 3) in part because it has received so much attention from others (e.g., Segal (1986), Gunderson (2003)), and also to make the point that Freudian reading can thrive independent of this topic.

knows or can imagine what it is like to mourn, and my exploration of the work of mourning in chapter 1 discovers a predictable set of emotions (grief, guilt, anger) coursing below the psychotextual surface. Though touching on far out fantasies, my discussion of motherhood in chapter 2 experiments with a psychoanalytic transformation of familiar critical practices. Chapter 3 presses the experiment further by taking up, and taking seriously, one of the least intuitively compelling of psychoanalytic stories (the castration complex) and, in a final section, parlaying this story into an irreducibly psychoanalytic mode of reading.

Because I am committed above all to psychoanalysis as an activity (not a set of concepts), I am interested in psychoanalytic themes only insofar as they arrive implicated in the textual unconscious, which means insofar as they appear to irrupt here and there into texts that cannot offer them official accommodation. This is why my chapter on mourning chiefly involves poems which pretend not to mourn; why my chapter on mothers attends to Dido more than Venus and to Philomela more than Procne; and why my chapter on the phallus focuses on Scylla instead of Iphis and on Berenice as much as Attis.

## In defense of the "as if"

Finally: if there is any one lesson to be learned from psychoanalysis, it is, or so I believe, that texts are not reducible to their "hidden meanings." To the contrary, texts accrue meaning by keeping their secrets secret.[27] Something essential is missed (to take a notorious pair of examples) in the critical tug-of-war over Catullus' *passer* poems (sparrow = penis, or sparrow = bird?) and his dinner invitation to Fabullus (perfume = "vaginal secretions," or perfume = perfume?).[28] If forced to choose, I will choose the non-obscene, literal interpretation: first, because Catullus is obviously ready to invoke the penis qua penis when that is what he means, and secondly, and more importantly, because bringing genitalia into these poems destroys their distinctive tone and texture. Yet

---

[27] A formulation that encapsulates my debt to Riffaterre and Shoptaw, both of whose theories, I should note, make space for psychoanalysis without giving it any special privilege (Riffaterre (1987) is not the Riffaterrean norm).

[28] On the *passer*, see further below, 123–4. The perfume is treated with appropriate tact by Fitzgerald (1995) 98–100.

the critics who harp on the genital allegory are responding to *something*, after all. The sparrow both answers and assuages the desire of Catullus' girlfriend; and the delectable, irresistible perfume, which will make Fabullus pray to be "all nose," is likewise hers, the gift of "Venus and her Cupids" (13.14, 12). These are poems of desire treating objects heavily freighted with desire, and these objects are erotic tokens that circulate among players (writer, reader, characters) of whatever sex. And this description is not a polite evasion of an underlying genital "truth." Sometimes fuzziness is more accurate – captures more of reality – than precision. So I hereby entreat my readers not simply to dismiss the qualifications that regularly attend my interpretations. The *as if*s and *almost*s and *effectively*s are not windowdressing but an indispensable part of the picture.

CHAPTER

# I

# Two poets mourning

Mourning is a topic upon which psychoanalysts and literary critics tend to converge. The convergence seems almost inevitable. Mourning happens – not exclusively, but crucially – in and through language; mourning may even be a constitutive feature of language, insofar as words are taken, according to the common nostalgic account, both to register and partly to make up for the loss of the things they name. From Freud's account of his grandson's attempts to master loss via the paradigmatic repetitions of the *fort/da* game, to Lacan's seminar on mourning in *Hamlet*, to Abraham and Torok's studies of melancholic incorporation as anti-metaphor, to Peter Sacks's psychogeneric reading of English elegy: to write about the "work of mourning" is to write about the mournful and melancholy words that help accomplish that work.[1]

Latin poetry offers its share of poems which participate in the praising, blaming, complaining, repetitious remembering, and aggressive forgetting that make up mourning.[2] Consider, for example, Horace's consolatory ode to Virgil on the death of Quintilius (*Carm.* 1.24), a poem that implicitly measures Horace's own austere performance of grief against what Horace represents, with howsoever little emphasis, as Virgil's excessive and irrational indulgence in mourning. The question that broaches the poem, "What restraint or limit should be set on our

---

[1] Freud (1920) 14–17, with Derrida (1987); Lacan ([1959] 1982); Abraham and Torok ([1972] 1994); Sacks (1985), all engaging with Freud (1917) (on the "work of mourning").

[2] Indeed, it is the Ovidian story of Apollo's loss and symbolic recuperation of Daphne that provides Sacks with his paradigm for "successful" mourning; see Sacks (1985) 4–5.

longing for so dear a friend?" (*Quis desiderio sit pudor aut modus | tam cari capitis?*, 1–2), is, it emerges, not just a rhetorical flourish. After memorializing the dead man's virtues (his moral restraint, trustworthiness, and adherence to "naked truth"), Horace remarks his particular intimacy with Virgil and then, in the pivotal central stanza, reproduces Virgil's ongoing complaint against the gods: "you, virtuous in vain, alas! demand Quintilius of the gods, not entrusted to them on these terms" (*tu frustra pius heu non ita creditum | poscis Quintilium deos*, 11–12). The final two stanzas comprise Horace's remonstrance: Virgil's sense of moral outrage is futile because death is final and total; not even if he could play more ravishingly than Orpheus himself could he conjure the blood back into the empty shade. Yet the poem's concluding lines resist this tough-minded lesson in the very act of driving it home: "It's hard; but patience renders easier to bear that which it is sin to correct" (*durum: sed levius fit patientia | quidquid corrigere est nefas*, 19–20). As Michael Putnam has pointed out, Quintilius is known to us from Horace's *Ars Poetica* as a vigilant and forthright critic (the virtues celebrated in this ode are likewise the critic's virtues), who could be counted on to say "correct this, please, and this" (*"corrige sodes | hoc" aiebat "et hoc,"* Ars 438–9). To chastise Virgil by describing death as beyond revision is to speak as Quintilius – even, as Putnam puts it, to reincarnate him.[3] Horace proves, then, to be no more resigned than Virgil to the loss of Quintilius. But his reaction is not to demand but simply to take Quintilius back, by building him into himself as part of a revised identity. The loss can (only?) be accepted because it has already, through introjection, been offset.[4]

Or again, take Catullus' elegiac farewell to his dead brother at the grave site in Asia to which he has made his pilgrimage. Andrew Feldherr has shown that this poem is rooted in the ritual deficiency that necessarily attends the man buried so far from home: no regularly recurring ceremonial practices will enable this dead man to come to rest within his

---

[3] Putnam (1993) 133–5. Whereas to ventriloquize Virgil is, within the context of this ode, to reject the *pudor* that distinguishes Quintilius, and ought to govern grief (especially among Epicureans; see Thibodeau (2003) 248–55).

[4] Cf. Freud (1923a) 28–30, where he recognizes the general operation of the preservative introjection he earlier associated with pathological melancholia.

community.[5] But for my purposes what is most striking about the poem is how very well it fulfills its impossible elegiac mission. Catullus has come on a long journey, he tells his brother, to pay him a final tribute and to address the tomb (*donarem, alloquerer*, 101.3, 4). And he proceeds to do just what he says he came to do – he makes his offering and speaks his piece (5–10):

> quandoquidem fortuna mihi tete abstulit ipsum,
>> heu miser indigne frater adempte mihi,
> nunc tamen interea haec, prisco quae more parentum
>> tradita sunt tristi munere ad inferias,
> accipe fraterno multum manantia fletu,
>> atque in perpetuum, frater, ave atque vale.

Since fortune has stolen your actual self away from me – alas, wretched brother wrongly taken from me! – now, even so, in the meantime, accept this offering, which the ancient custom of our ancestors has handed down as a sad gift to the spirits below, soaked with a brother's abundant tears, and forevermore, brother, hail and farewell.

The poem does a most thorough job of mourning. Grief and anger receive their due (the exclamatory *heu*, the resentful *indigne*) before giving place to the consolation of ancestral tradition, which extends the individual life into the past and (by implication) the future. But all this happens within the subordinate clauses. The essential burden of the poem is carried by the imperatives, *accipe* and *ave atque vale*, which bracket the brother, ritually invoked for the third and last time, in their embrace.

Indeed, the performance is almost too efficient, the seal almost too tight, as if the poem meant to put an end to the brother once and for all. Whereas Horace keeps Quintilius alive by introjecting his critical voice, this elegy seems to be haunted by the converse possibility: that the survivor's identification with the dead will pull him down into darkness, barrenness, speechlessness. The danger is encapsulated in lines 3–4, "to give you the final offering due to death, and to speak in vain to the mute ash" (*ut te postremo donarem munere mortis / et mutam nequiquam alloquerer cinerem*), where the contrast between "you" and "ash" corresponds to the fullness and emptiness of the speech each elicits: on one side, the

---

[5] Feldherr (2000), including a dazzling discussion of the confusion of brothers, on which I draw below.

expressive sonority of the hexameter addressing "you"; on the other, the ironic self-muting of the pentameter, its elided, mutilated *nequiquam* suggesting that the language of the living brother is being infiltrated by the silence of the dead one. No wonder, then, that there immediately follows the poem's most extended apostrophe, which is to say its most vivid realization of voice. The dangerous interchangeability of the dead and living brothers is what the poem both communicates and forestalls.

Much has been written and more could be written about poems such as these, which may not require the attentions of psychoanalysis, but do respond interestingly to them. Yet though the emotions that agitate these poems will recur throughout this chapter, elegy proper is not my subject here. In the poems sampled above, mourning is on the official agenda; it is what the poems are designed to do. But what will engage me in this chapter is the way mourning infiltrates, as if without the mourner's knowledge or consent, texts which are not officially "elegiac" at all. These elegies *malgré soi* will enable me to delve further into the psychotextuality of mourning while also beginning to make a case for the interpretive value of what I am calling the textual unconscious, not as the goal but as a means of reading: a postulate that renders the wrinkles and rifts in the surface visible, and makes them matter.

The mourners on whom I will concentrate are Catullus in his long poems[6] (in particular, the two awkwardly known as 65 and 68b) and Orpheus in the tenth book of Ovid's *Metamorphoses*. Readers will notice the discrepancy: the one a poet, the other a character in a poet's fiction. The point of the juxtaposition is not to flatten Catullus into "Catullus," a character in a fiction composed by an author who happens to bear the same name. Still less do I plan to treat Ovid's Orpheus as a person possessed of a psyche and history to which Ovid's poem affords us unimpeded access. It is just that this juxtaposition helps me bring into focus various issues – intentionality, intertextuality, self-reflexivity – that

---

[6] While there is good reason to believe in the existence of (some form of) polymetric and elegiac *libelli*, there is no external evidence that 61–8 circulated together; see Hutchinson (2003) 209–11; Butrica (2007) 19–24. Still, the thematic coherence of 61–4 has persuaded many readers that these at least must have formed their own book; see, e.g., Holzberg (2002) 111–50. Here and in chapter 3, my minimal presupposition is that, regardless of their publication history, the long poems are deep in conversation with each other. On the general issue of Catullan book design, see now Skinner (2007a).

have a bearing on how "we Latinists" read. Recently Stephen Hinds has explored the virtual poles of "philological fundamentalism" and "intertextualist fundamentalism" (with their respective commitments to authorial "allusions" and authorless "intertexts") and has made the case for allowing interpretation to travel along the continuum that stretches from the one position to the other.[7] This chapter extends Hinds's argument by focusing on knots in the continuum: places where the "unintended" can be productively described as, precisely, *not* intended, *contrary* to intention, and hence the sign of another, seemingly alien intention.

## The death of Eurydice and the song of Orpheus

It has long since been recognized that Ovid is interested in why storytellers tell the stories they do – in their nondisinterestedness, so to put it, whether rhetorical (tailored to a particular audience) or (wittingly or unwittingly) confessional.[8] Ovid seems positively to invite us to dig up the "hidden motivations" with which he has obligingly stocked his characters in advance. A familiar instance is the song performed by Ovid's Orpheus in *Metamorphoses* 10. On the one hand, Orpheus is an authorial surrogate who picks up the narrative thread and contributes his share of material (Hyacinth, Pygmalion, Myrrha, Adonis, Atalanta) to the metamorphic theme. On the other hand, as Eleanor Winsor Leach, Micaela Janan, and Philip Hardie have variously shown, for all its superficial impersonality and narrative transparency, the song can also be read as a work of mourning, intimately bound to the recent history of the twice-bereaved singer.[9] This is particularly clear in the story of the sculptor Pygmalion, who, horrified by the vices of contemporary womankind, falls in love with the ideal woman he has fashioned out of ivory, and ends up (with Venus' help) enjoying her in the flesh. The fact that this story so signally departs from the synopsis Orpheus provided before launching into his song – he had promised stories of "boys loved by the gods" and "girls smitten with forbidden flames" (10.152–4) – already points to an ulterior pressure at work. As Leach remarks, "the story appears

---

[7] Hinds (1998) ch. 2.     [8] A succinct and suggestive account in Barchiesi (2002).

[9] Leach (1974); Janan (1988); Hardie (2002) 65–70 (the song as "a concatenation of tales of desire and loss that strive to offer textual substitutes for the irreplaceable lack caused by the death of Eurydice," 68).

to serve as Orpheus' own wish-projection": where the singer ultimately failed to reanimate his beloved, the sculptor succeeds in bringing his life-like artwork to life.[10] In a kind of replication of the logic of the Pygmalion story, Orpheus consoles himself for the inadequacy of his "real-life" experience by creating an ideal fiction of artistic and erotic success.

The psychobiographical reading of Orpheus' Pygmalion is so compel-ling that readers have tended not to remark at what pains Ovid has been to obscure the connections on which it is founded. Far from painting Orpheus as a bereaved husband, Ovid repeatedly indicates that the singer is long since done with mourning. After his second and final loss of Eurydice, Orpheus concentrates his grief into seven days spent fasting and suing for passage back into the underworld (a few decades earlier, the Orpheus of Virgil's *Georgics* had mourned for seven months!). Thereafter he withdraws into the mountains of Thrace, whence he shuns the love of women and even (*etiam*, 10.83, as if taking his revulsion the next logical step) teaches his fellow countrymen the superior merits of boys (it is Orpheus, Ovid tells us, who introduced pederasty into Thrace). When he takes his seat on a hilltop in preparation for the performance that will fill the rest of *Metamorphoses* 10, a full three years have elapsed since Eurydice's death, and her loss is so remote that Orpheus can contrast his new "lighter" theme (*leviore lyra*, 152) not with heavy-hearted elegiac lamentation, but with the "weightier strain" of the grand epic he was wont to perform (*cecini plectro graviore Gigantas*, 152). Everything here con-spires to suggest that the dead wife has been successfully forgotten.

I stress the overtly un-mournful cast of the song not to refute the mournful reading, but because it matters to me that the narrative surface cleaves so resolutely to Orpheus' consciousness – that of a man who has come out on the other side of mourning. This alliance is not just a matter of narrative technique, showing versus telling. To the contrary, when it comes to the mournful dimension of Orpheus' song, the narrator (not the author; here the two do, I think, part company)[11] seems as willfully

---

[10] Leach (1974) 123.

[11] This claim may seem bizarre, but readers of Ovid are actually accustomed to such divergences. Cf. the series of stories of gods chasing nymphs in *Met.* 1, where the narrator (moving by an associative logic from one story to the next) seems quite unaware of the obvious thematic connections; the author, however, famously acknowledges the monotony by feeding it back into the story (the third time around, this theme puts Argus to sleep).

innocent as his character. This innocence, or better complicity, is evident from the outset. Orpheus failed to bring Eurydice back to life, not because of a flaw in his art (his song did earn Eurydice's release), but because he violated the one condition (*legem*, 10.50) laid upon him by the gods of the underworld, "that he not turn his eyes back" before emerging (*ne flectat retro sua lumina*, 51). Eurydice's relapse is thus, it would appear, not just Orpheus' failure but Orpheus' fault. Yet even as Orpheus looks back, the narrator intercedes with an exculpatory qualification: "fearing lest she fail, and greedy for a look, he turned (loving her as he did) his eyes, and at once she slipped back ..." (*hic ne deficeret metuens avidusque videndi* / *flexit* **amans** *oculos, et protinus illa relapsa est*, 56–7). Eurydice herself, the narrator insists, was bound to second this sympathetic judgment (60–3):

> iamque iterum moriens non est de coniuge quidquam
> questa suo (quid enim nisi se quereretur amatam?)
> supremumque "vale," quod iam vix auribus ille
> acciperet, dixit revolutaque rursus eodem est.

And now, dying for a second time, she uttered no complaint about her husband (for of what could she have complained, besides being loved?) and said a last "farewell," which by now he could scarcely hear, and spiraled back down again to the same place.

As commentators note, the narrator is going out of his way here to correct Virgil, whose Eurydice does indeed reproach her husband before slipping away forever (*Geo.* 4.494–8):

> illa "quis et me" inquit "miseram et te perdidit, Orpheu,
> quis tantus furor? en iterum crudelia retro
> fata vocant, conditque natantia lumina somnus.
> iamque vale: feror ingenti circumdata nocte
> invalidasque tibi tendens, heu non tua, palmas."

"Why have you destroyed me," said she, "poor me, and yourself too, Orpheus? What irresistible madness is this? Look, the cruel fates summon me back again, and sleep shrouds my swimming eyes. Now farewell: vast night surrounds me, and I am carried off, reaching out strengthless hands to you, alas, yours no more."

Of this plangent accusation Ovid retains but the one colorless word *vale*, "farewell." Still, if his Eurydice utters no reproaches, she has no comfort to offer either. It is not she but the narrator who makes the case for Orpheus.[12] Though the narrator covers for her (she is whisked away instantly, *protinus* – no time for even a single hexameter!), the effect is as of discourse censored. It is as if, having nothing nice to say, Ovid's Eurydice were reduced to saying nothing at all.

Ovid's Orpheus, then, has nothing to reproach himself with. So says the narrator, and Eurydice does not (or is not allowed to) contradict him. And yet, far from successfully erasing the Virgilian Eurydice's reproach, the narrator's negation only intensifies its influence upon the ensuing narrative; his "not guilty," with all its attendant paranoia of guilt, will be repeated, again and again, by Orpheus himself. The verdict will moreover be backed up, quite as usual, by the ascription of guilt to another, *the* other, the wronged other – here, Eurydice in her surrogates.[13] This two-pronged strategy of exoneration appears at its most abstract in Orpheus' initial summary of his twofold theme: "boys loved by the gods" and "girls who, smitten with forbidden flames, merited punishment for their lust" (*puerosque ... | dilectos superis inconcessisque puellas | ignibus attonitas meruisse libidine poenam*, 10.152–4). The subject matter has obvious links to the new erotic inclinations of the singer. Earlier the narrator had ascribed this sexual reorientation either to Orpheus' prior heterosexual misfortune, or to a pledge of fidelity to Eurydice (a pledge that keeps him, it seems, only from loving another *woman*). But what Orpheus' emphasis on crime and punishment suggests is that his turn away from women is a consequence of his finding, and needing to find, women guilty – very, *very* guilty. His paired themes are, it emerges, complementary: whereas the female sex is guilt-laden (and by implication hated by the gods), the male sex is loved by the gods (and by implication guilt-free). In the event, this antithesis will be complicated by others: god vs. mortal, lover vs. beloved.[14]

---

[12] Contrast Virgil's Creusa, a Eurydice who explicitly exonerates her "Orpheus" (in Aeneas' version of the story!) at the end of *Aeneid* 2.

[13] On the narrator's complicity and Orpheus' guilt (and misogyny), see Cahoon (2005).

[14] And also complicated in the narrative event, most notably with Myrrha. Though the teller insists in the strongest of terms on her extreme guilt, the tale largely exonerates her, so effectively, in fact, that the self-condemning Myrrha emerges as one of the most sympathetic figures in the poem. Thus Orpheus' fierce revulsion begins to seem like overmuch protesting, as if Myrrha answered to the artist's narcissistic passion for his creations. On the multiple ironies surrounding this episode, see Barchiesi (2001) 56–62.

But however the story plays out, guilt regularly adheres to the position Orpheus does not occupy.

Complicit as ever, the narrator offers examples of the same strategy before Orpheus even strikes up his song. Consider the otherwise unknown story of boastful Lethaea and her doting husband Olenos, who tried to save his wicked wife by assuming her guilt (*quique in se crimen traxit voluitque videri / Olenos esse nocens*, 10.68–9) but succeeded only in sharing her punishment. Smuggled into the simile describing Orpheus' stupefaction at Eurydice's second death, the story registers as a tendentious gesture toward exculpation, with Olenos a whitewashed Orpheus and Lethaea a blackened Eurydice.[15] It is as if, for the narrator as for Orpheus, somehow or other the wife *must* be to blame. Again, take the story of Cyparissus, which is told by the narrator (the cypress is the last mentioned of the trees that, drawn by the Orphic lyre, provide the singer with shade[16]) but would have been quite at home within Orpheus' song. Cyparissus was once a boy cherished by Apollo (*puer ... deo dilectus*, 107, like the boys Orpheus is about to hymn), himself in turn passionately attached to his bejeweled pet stag. Hunting one day at the fatal hour of noon, the boy unwittingly (*imprudens*, 130) pierces his pet with a javelin. Though Apollo applies both comfort and admonition, advising him to "grieve in moderation, and in proportion to the object" (*ut leviter pro materiaque doleret*, 133), Cyparissus remains inconsolable, and Apollo finally grants his wish by transforming him into his namesake: sad cypress, the ever-grieving funereal tree. Here is no doubt a guilty lover. Yet the beloved he has done to death is after all only a pet, hardly meriting so much passion, whether of affection or of grief; an exemplary contrast is provided by Apollo's notably restrained grief (a mere couplet, 141–2) at the consequent loss of his own lovable human "pet," Cyparissus. Whereas Olenos is hyper-innocent, the crime of Cyparissus is too trivial to merit prosecution.

It is in the first extended episode of his song that Orpheus works through the question of guilt most elaborately.[17] This is the story of

---

[15] Cf. Anderson (1972) 481.

[16] *umbra loco deerat* (10.88); as soon as Orpheus sweeps his strings, shade (a troop of trees) dutifully appears (*umbra loco venit*, 90). But the humor turns black when we recollect the other missing "shade" that this song will not succeed in summoning.

[17] Well discussed, with a different emphasis, by Janan (1988) 117–24.

Hyacinth, another of Apollo's favorites. It is noon again, and the lovers, taking a break from hunting, are playing at discus-toss, when the discus hurled by Apollo takes a fatal bounce, striking Hyacinth in the face. Earlier it was Cyparissus who was *imprudens* when he threw the javelin that killed his pet stag. Here it is not the lover but his pet, not Apollo but Hyacinth, rushing to pick up the discus, who is *imprudens* and even *actus ... cupidine lusus*, "driven by his eagerness for the game" (10.182). With Cyparissus, I rendered *imprudens* as "unwittingly"; with Hyacinth, a harsher translation such as "reckless" is in order. My point is that Orpheus is exculpating Apollo in advance by laying the blame for the tragedy on Hyacinth's own impatience. Apollo does not let himself off so easily, however: "In your wound I see my crime, you are my sorrow and my sin, it is my right hand that will be inscribed with your death! I am the author of your end!" (197–9). Yet having thus as it were gotten the guilt out of his system, Apollo proceeds (like many another distressed Ovidian soliloquizer, but with better justification, as it seems) to ease his moral discomfort by reasoning himself into a more satisfactory view of his case: "All the same, what *is* my guilt? unless it can be called 'guilt' to have played, 'guilt' even to have loved" (*quae mea culpa tamen? nisi si lusisse vocari / culpa potest, nisi culpa potest et amasse vocari*, 200–1). The mild non sequitur of *et amasse* (it was Apollo's play, not his love, that killed Hyacinth) has aroused editorial suspicions (and this pair of lines is bracketed by Tarrant). But the "interpolation" is intraOvidian, as it were, inserted by the internal narrator, to whose case *et amasse* exactly applies. Thus by way of Apollo Orpheus makes in full and at reasonably satisfying length the confession of guilt he never made in person. Yet also by way of Apollo he empties his confession of all but emotional truth. How can we fault Apollo, really, if his reckless beloved rushed headlong into the rebounding discus? It is not by chance, moreover, that Orpheus ascribes to Hyacinth an impatience reminiscent of his own fatal haste – a projection of blame from lover to beloved fueled by the very impossibility of holding Eurydice accountable for her own death.

At the very end of his song, after rehearsing Pygmalion's happily resolved obsession with his ivory image, and his great-granddaughter Myrrha's tragic love for her father (his prime example of a wicked girl undone by forbidden desire), Orpheus returns to the theme of "boys loved by the gods" with the story of the beautiful Adonis, the darling of

Venus (and the very image of her son Cupid; the incest continues ... ).[18] Into this tale Orpheus inserts another, the story of Atalanta and Hippomenes, which Venus tells Adonis, purportedly to dissuade him from hunting dangerous animals, such as the lions into which these lovers were eventually transformed. As far as Venus is concerned, the story is a failure; Adonis, not dissuaded, will shortly be killed by a boar, and thereafter, like Hyacinth at the start of the song, honored with a festival and transformed into a flower (so ends *Metamorphoses* 10).[19] But the tale Venus tells serves other purposes for Orpheus. He must have a particular interest, for example, in its surpassingly swift-footed heroine Atalanta (*passu ... alite*, 10.587). When last seen, his Eurydice was limping, her pace slowed by her ankle wound (*passu de vulnere tardo*, 49). Perhaps it was Eurydice's tardiness that precipitated Orpheus' disastrous impatience; it must have taken so long to travel the upward path out of the underworld! Yet here the roles have been exchanged (and normalized), so that it is the swift woman who races ahead, the tardy lover who follows behind. If anyone is guilty here, it is not Hippomenes but Atalanta, she who consigns her slow-footed suitors to death, and who contemplates, and uneasily dismisses, the question of her own culpability: "but it is not my fault!" (*sed non culpa mea est*, 629, echoing Apollo's exculpatory rhetoric at 200–1). In this case, however, there really will be no trace of blood on her hands, or on his: Atalanta doesn't bring about the death of Hippomenes (he wins his race), and Hippomenes doesn't bring about the death of Atalanta (unlike Hyacinth – the contrast seems marked – she is not injured when she rushes to pick up the bouncing missiles hurled by her lover).[20]

Hippomenes is thus, like Pygmalion, a wishful projection, an improved image of Orpheus: a blameless man who braves death to win a wife, and wins her indeed. But the happy ending toward which the story seems headed is forestalled, since (as the narrating Venus intervenes to point out, with high indignation) Hippomenes neglected to pay the helpful goddess, who answered his prayers by ensuring his victory, the thanks that were her due (*dignane, cui grates ageret ...? / nec grates immemor egit*, 10.681–2); this oversight leads somewhat circuitously to the lovers' being transformed into lions in the service of the goddess Cybele. Did Orpheus

---

[18] Hardie (2002) 186–8.    [19] Hardie (2002) 69.
[20] Verbal echoes (*misit, cupidine, tollere*, etc.) reinforce the obvious thematic connections.

perchance likewise forget to thank the underworld gods for yielding to his entreaties and giving him back his wife? Certainly someone, either the Ovidian narrator or Orpheus himself, omitted the display of gratitude we and the gods might have expected. Could it be that this failure of basic good manners is the reason Orpheus lost Eurydice the second time? A notable contrast is provided by the uniquely happy Pygmalion, who returns instant and superabundant thanks to Venus upon gaining a wife (*plenissima ... / verba, quibus Veneri grates agit*, 290–1). Yet if the oversight Orpheus nowhere avows finds expression, so near the end of his song, in Hippomenes, everything else seems to be moving toward the exoneration of the bereaved lover: from Orpheus' guilt, to Apollo's proximate responsibility, to Venus' mere absenting of herself – hardly a blameworthy action, especially given that she has done her best to fortify her beloved against the lurking dangers of the hunt before she takes her leave. And in the event Venus blames not herself (nor, for that matter, her rash beloved) but the fates (*questaque cum fatis*, 724), as Orpheus, albeit with less justice, earlier blamed not himself (nor the unarguably blameless Eurydice) but the unbending gods of the underworld (*esse deos Erebi crudeles questus*, 76), for refusing him passage back across the Styx. When Venus, sailing off in her chariot toward Cyprus, catches Adonis' death groan, she reins around her swans, *flexit aves* (720), as Orpheus before turned his gaze, *flexit amans oculos* (57). In this case one can only wish the lover had turned back sooner. Orpheus thus finally recasts his murderous transgression as benevolent concern: the backward-turning mindfulness conveyed by the verb *respicere*.[21]

## Catullus in mourning

The relation between Ovid and Orpheus is relatively simple. Ovid is the knowing author, Orpheus the blinkered character, who nowhere recognizes but intermittently betrays his personal investment in his song. The relation between Catullus the poet and "Catullus" the speaker of poems 65 and 68b is more difficult to disentangle. Though I will sometimes point to places where I think we have reason to think that Catullus and "Catullus" either converge or diverge, my only definite claim about the

---

[21] Which finally surfaces to seal Orpheus' story at 11.66: *Eurydicenque suam iam tuto respicit Orpheus.*

author–persona relation is that it is more likely to fluctuate than to remain constant. This is true even of the relation of Ovid to Orpheus. Though Ovid may know Orpheus better than he (Ovid or Orpheus) can know himself, he does not keep at a consistent distance from his character, or (to put it from the reader's side) the interpretive pay-off of remarking this distance (or, conversely, of occluding this distance by identifying the one poet with the other) varies from line to line and episode to episode. In any case, I do not want or need to claim that every detail I have fixed on was "planted" there by Ovid just for the sake of a reading such as mine. It may be that the resemblance I detect between Atalanta and Hyacinth had, for Ovid, quite another value.[22] Still, it is only Orpheus' manufactured unconscious that I have been venturing to plumb. Now, though, I am turning my attention to a character who shares a name if not a psyche with the author.

The intertwining of Catullus with "Catullus" in poems 65 and 68b is intensified, moreover, by the opacity and waywardness, the relative unreadability, of these poems. It may be a carefully contrived authorial effect, but everything takes place as if the perversely extended similes that are the most striking feature of these poems had a life and a communicative energy of their own. It is true that Catullus, unlike Orpheus, knows (even insists) that he is still mourning: mourning the brother to whom he dedicates the formal elegiac tribute of poem 101. That elegy ends, as we have seen, with a famous speech act: "forevermore, brother, hail and farewell" (101.10). But in the poems I am looking at here, whether because they fall earlier in the quasi-autobiographical chronology of the collection, or for other reasons still to be explored, the closural "farewell" has not (yet) sealed the tomb. Whereas conventional elegies are supposed to carry us through the phases of mourning (disbelief, anger, grief, resignation) so as to release us on the other side, these poems catch Catullus ("Catullus"?) in the anguished middle, half-remembering, or half-forgetting.[23]

Partly because of their uneasy commingling of author and character, memory and forgetting, these poems have posed a special challenge to

---

[22] E.g., as an index of their shared kinship with Daphne, whom the boastful suitor Apollo (an unsuccessful Hippomenes) signally fails to overtake in the race of *Met.* 1. On Apollo's pet "plants," Daphne and Hyacinth, see Hardie (2002) 64.

[23] This is what Derrida (1987) 335 refers to as "midmourning."

their scholarly interpreters. Whereas my reading of Orpheus harmonized, in outline if not in detail, with the work of scholars such as Janan and Hardie, my reading of Catullus is more deviant. It is designed to show the benefits of attending to the textual unconscious of poems 65 and 68b – the textual unconscious, as opposed to the poetic self-consciousness which has so fascinated Catullus' readers.

## Forgotten fruit

The textual unconscious of poem 65 is produced in the interstices of its orderly syntax. The poem is framed as a letter to Hortalus, who has (we learn) requested some poetry from Catullus; Catullus replies, in a single sentence elaborated across twelve couplets, that despite his overwhelming grief, which renders him incapable of creation, he is indeed sending Hortalus some poetry, a translation from Callimachus (i.e., poem 66, a translation of Callimachus' fanciful, courtly "Lock of Berenice," to which this cover letter is as it were attached). This, the gist of the letter, is amplified by two extrusions. The first is a recollection of his brother's death, inserted by way of explanation after the opening concessive clause (65.1–8):

> Etsi me assiduo confectum cura dolore
>  sevocat a doctis, Ortale, virginibus,
> nec potis est dulcis Musarum expromere fetus
>  mens animi, tantis fluctuat ipsa malis –
> namque mei nuper Lethaeo gurgite fratris
>  pallidulum manans alluit unda pedem,
> Troia Rhoeteo quem subter litore tellus
>  ereptum nostris obterit ex oculis.

Though distress keeps me, overwhelmed by constant grief, from the well-schooled maidens, Hortalus, and my mind cannot bring forth the sweet fruits of the Muses, tossed as it is on such vast waves of trouble – for it was but lately that my brother's pallid foot was washed by the current of Lethe's stream, my brother, who, stolen from my sight, lies crushed by Trojan earth near the Rhoetean shore.

This explanation in turn opens the door to a full-fledged apostrophe (10–14):[24]

---

[24] A hexameter is missing from the transmitted text.

> numquam ego te, vita frater amabilior,
> aspiciam posthac? at certe semper amabo,
>   semper maesta tua carmina morte canam,
> qualia sub densis ramorum concinit umbris
>   Daulias, absumpti fata gemens Ityli. –

Shall I never look upon you henceforth, brother more beloved than life? Yet surely will I ever love you, ever sing songs made mournful by your death, such as beneath the clustered shadows of branches the Daulian sings, grieving the fate of Itylus undone. –

The mournful digression is then sealed off by a resumptive return to Hortalus and the long-postponed delivery of the poem's main verb: "but all the same, Hortalus, even in the midst of such overwhelming sorrows, I am sending ..." (*sed tamen in tantis maeroribus, Ortale, mitto*, 15). The seal is indeed so tight – the contrast between sentence and parenthesis, letter and lament, so marked – that the outburst comes to appear mounted as a specimen of mourning, mentioned more than used. The distinction between Catullus the writing author and "Catullus" the exclamatory stage mourner comes into focus in the telltale shift from *nuper* to *semper*: whereas Catullus excuses his distraction by pleading the recency of the loss, "Catullus" laments in a timeless zone where wounds never heal.

Yet the ostentatious demonstration of grief itself becomes the vehicle of other, less fully acknowledged emotions. In Catullus' miniature epic on the marriage of Peleus and Thetis, with its long inset ecphrasis on the plight of Ariadne abandoned by Theseus, Ariadne describes her *quondam* lover as "a young man spattered with a brother's blood" (*respersum iuvenem fraterna caede*, 64.181; the blood of her "brother" the Minotaur, she means), and the narrator likewise singles out, as the first horror of the postlapsarian world, the crime of fratricide, "brothers [with] hands soaked in brothers' blood" (*perfudere manus fraterno sanguine fratres*, 399). It is as if the brother of poem 65 were likewise not just dead but murdered, his blood on Catullus' hands. As Marilyn Skinner has pointed out, the "Rhoetean" grave site is renowned chiefly as the burial place of the hero Ajax, whose brother, the hapless Teucer, survived to be blamed and banished by his angry father; and the "Daulian" nightingale sings in perpetual mourning for a son she herself killed.[25]

---

[25] Skinner (2003) 5–14.

That Catullus feels the painful pressure of the latter image is suggested by his breaking off his apostrophe just where he does. The passive participle *absumpti* ("destroyed," "consumed") is reticent about assigning responsibility for the fate of Itylus. But in the Homeric prototype of this simile, the phrase "grieving for her dear child Itylus" is followed by the shocking "whom she killed with a sword" (Homer *Od.* 19.522–3).

If Lethe marks the threshold between the upper and underworlds, it is because the dead have to be forgotten so that the living can continue to live. Yet for the mourner, forgetting is a culpable perfidy, tantamount to murder; it is letting the lost one slip away, once again, into the dark. (Returning to Orpheus, we might say that it is his inability to "see" Eurydice when she is not before his eyes – his failure to keep her image before him – that produces his fatal, literalistic turn.) In his miniature epic, Catullus lays down an emphatic contrast between memory and forgetfulness: whereas Ariadne ignores the waves lapping at the clothing that has slipped down to her feet (*ipsius ante pedes fluctus salis*, 64.67), entirely preoccupied as she is with, even obsessed by, her departing lover (69–70), Theseus is above all *immemor*, the very embodiment of obliviousness.[26] In the letter to Hortalus, Catullus plays both parts: devoted to his dead brother, keeping him continually in view, and yet sailing away, abandoning him at the lapping margin of Lethe, back into the claims of life, embodied here by the request of his eminent friend. Thus the extravagant tribute to his brother may be paid precisely *to* his brother, as if in answer to a ghostly reproach: how can Catullus occupy his thoughts with Hortalus and poetry, his brother so recently dead?

It is as if, the tribute thus paid in full, and safely deposited at the very center of the poem, Catullus were free to turn his mind toward what he owes Hortalus. In the final couplets, it is his good credit not with his brother but with Hortalus that is at issue, and it is this that generates the second of the two syntactical extrusions to which I referred at the outset, here a single, brilliantly extended simile (65.15–24):

---

[26] *immemor*, 64.58; *immemori ... pectore*, 123; *immemor*, 135; *oblito ... pectore*, 208; *mente immemori*, 248; see also 64.231-2, 238–40.

sed tamen in tantis maeroribus, Ortale, mitto
    haec expressa tibi carmina Battiadae,
ne tua dicta vagis nequiquam credita ventis
    effluxisse meo forte putes animo,
ut missum sponsi furtivo munere malum
    procurrit casto virginis e gremio
quod miserae oblitae molli sub veste locatum,
    dum adventu matris prosilit, excutitur,
atque illud prono praeceps agitur decursu,
    huic manat tristi conscius ore rubor.

But even so, in the midst of this overwhelming sorrow, Hortalus, I send you this translation of Callimachus, lest perchance you should think your words, entrusted in vain to the shifting winds, have slipped my mind, as when an apple, sent as a lover's secret gift, rolls out of a maiden's innocent lap, the apple she put, poor forgetful thing, under her delicate dress, and which is shaken out when she jumps up at her mother's approach; and it races headlong in slanting downward course, while she feels the conscious blush wash across her sad cheeks.

The initial point of comparison is underscored by the similar shape of the quasi-rhyming pentameter lines 18 and 20, with their parallel verbs and symmetrically disposed ablatives: *effluxisse meo forte putes animo, procurrit casto virginis e gremio*. The simile illustrates the reproach Catullus is forestalling: the apple tumbles from the forgetful girl's lap, but [Hortalus is not to think that] his words have slipped Catullus' mind. Yet though the local context underwrites this interpretation, the poem as a whole opens up other possibilities. One upon which critics have fastened with particular enthusiasm is the self-reflexive correspondence between the maiden with her apple and the "sweet fruit" (= poetry) of the "maiden" Muses (2–3) from whom Catullus claimed to be alienated in the poem's opening lines. The simile thus becomes the vehicle of a "covert self-referentiality": the poem tumbles into view like the apple from the girl's lap, and Catullus succeeds as if despite himself in producing poetry, as per Hortalus' request.[27] The paradox – the apple as an image of a disavowed forgetfulness, the apple as the evidence of a dutiful mindfulness – is perhaps mitigated by the Callimachean flavor of

---

[27] Skinner (2003) 14.

the vividly realized vignette,[28] which offers a kind of preview of what Hortalus can expect from Catullus' engagement with Callimachus.

I do not deny that the poem has a self-reflexive dimension (it is after all "about" poetry). But in this case (and even more so in 68b, as we will see) scholarly satisfaction with the self-reflexive reading tends to warp the poem and block its circulating energies. As William Fitzgerald has stressed, this poem is permeated by the figuration of pregnancy, from the *fetus* ("fruit," but also "offspring") Catullus' preoccupied mind is incapable of yielding, to the telltale proof of guilty knowledge that tumbles from the girl's *gremium* ("lap," but also "womb"). "The metaphor of pregnancy," Fitzgerald observes, "makes the demands placed on Catullus by the two men incompatible: either he forgets his brother or he lets the words of Ortalus from his mind."[29] It is true that Catullus directly confronts this conflict, insofar as he represents translation as a compromise, a way of satisfying Hortalus without forgoing his grief – as if the labor of translation (as opposed to creation) bypassed the grieving mind, leaving it still pregnant with the image of his dead brother. Yet the compromise only substitutes one displacement for another. Made to speak again in Catullus' translation, and thus as it were brought back from the dead, the Greek poet effectively takes the place of the "mute ash" (101.4) of the dead brother. It is to Callimachus that the translator remains faithful; it is his instantly recognizable image that Catullus, like a chaste wife, delivers whole to posterity.[30]

Thus the Callimachean apple bears the burden not just of the poem but of the forgetting that is entailed in producing the poem: the apple carries (the aborted memory, the cast-off image of) the brother.[31] The guiltily blushing girl with the "innocent lap" resembles not only the virginal muses but also the bloodspattered nightingale, endlessly lamenting the

---

[28] Skinner (2003) 15–18.  [29] Fitzgerald (1995) 194.

[30] Cf. the *parvulus Torquatus* of poem 61.209, a faithful reproduction of the father's name and image via the blank maternal medium.

[31] Though everything in his discussion is moving toward this conclusion (see Fitzgerald (1995) 192–4), Fitzgerald never takes this step, perhaps because he is committed to the self-reflexive image of apple-as-poem, which he takes to be the prima facie meaning of the simile. Cf. Quinn (1972) 264 on the "beautiful and unexpected simile, in which the translation is likened to an apple given to a girl as a secret gift."

child she murdered.[32] Her violent parting from the figurative child "shaken out" of her lap is registered in the branching alternatives of the final couplet: one fate for the apple (*illud*, 23), rolling away beyond recall, and another for the girl (*huic*, 24) left behind to grieve. The blush that turns her "sad face" into an image of the conventionally ruddy-cheeked apple is her mournful attempt to incorporate the lost object, to catch it up again and so preserve it.

It matters, for my reading, that the meanings of the simile are not on an equal footing (as it were jostling for dominion) but organized in a kind of hierarchy. The "official" task assigned to the simile, as syntax, diction, and the run of the thought conspire to make clear, is to illustrate, by contrast with the girl "forgetful" of what she harbors in her lap, Catullus' non-forgetfulness of the *dicta* Hortalus has entrusted to his mind. It is only by stepping back and looking at the poem as a whole that readers apprehend the association of the forgotten apple with the poetic "fruit" that demonstrates Catullus' mindfulness. This paradox can be recuperated as a graceful irony, whereby authorial omniscience (Catullus sees and foreknows the whole poem, including the correspondence of Muses' to maiden's fruit) subsumes the partial knowledge of the Catullan speaker. Yet the forgetfulness embodied in the apple cannot but resurface, since remembering Hortalus with a poem means letting the brother's image slip away. It may be that Catullus the author is perfectly in control of the guiltily belated recollection of his brother that is written into this simile. But what matters for my purposes is that everything takes place as if the simile took Catullus as unawares as the apple takes the girl. Whereas the mournful lament that spills out of the center of the poem gave us a Catullus who seemed to know almost too well what he was about, the power of the simile derives from its apparent waywardness. The lament loudly insists that Catullus remembers his brother. But the simile itself guiltily and belatedly remembers.

## About the mistress: the gossip of the page

Catullus 68b is one of the strangest poems, I would almost venture to say *the* strangest poem, to come down to us from antiquity. Whereas

---

[32] In *casto* one feels the exculpatory pressure of the mourner's "not guilty": like Teucer, and like Catullus, the maiden is innocent of any real crime (I owe this observation to Corinne Crawford).

65 tethers its simile to the hypotactic framework of the sentence, the sixty couplets that compose 68b ("b" because this poem is preceded by and in the manuscripts joined to a cover letter, conventionally numbered 68a)[33] are almost entirely taken over by similes. Bizarre similes, too, piled one upon another, and so bewilderingly elaborated that the prima facie meaning sometimes remains a matter of dispute.[34] This "early experiment in stream of consciousness technique" (Kenneth Quinn's phrase) produces a poem ripe, as it seems, for psychoanalysis.[35] Yet though psychoanalytic critics such as Paul Allen Miller and Micaela Janan have written extensively and suggestively about poem 68b, they are, by and large, uninterested in listening for the unconscious that might be heard speaking in or through the wayward textual surface, focusing by preference on a Lacanian thematics (for Miller, the interplay of Symbolic and Imaginary; for Janan, the nature of desire) that the poem can be taken to illustrate.[36] It is true that the waywardness of 68b appears to be strictly controlled. As Quinn has pointed out, the "stream of consciousness" courses through an elaborate poetic design: like poem 65, albeit on a much larger scale, poem 68b is highly structured, with several sets of symmetrical panels framing its central elegiac divagation.[37] Insofar as readers take this design (the caveats of theorists notwithstanding) as evidence of the controlling intention of an artist, they are likely to refrain from speculating about what slips through the meshes, or better (since the question is less what gets out of the poem than everything that gets in) what worms its way in through the seams. As J. P. Elder long ago remarked in an elegant parenthesis, contemplating the architecture seems to entail forgetting the materials of the poem:

> (For the moment one forgets the diverse elements which have here their uneasy *rendezvous* – the gobs and chunks of poetry, the outrageously long and often unclear comparisons ... All these lie

---

[33] My working assumption is that 68a and b are yoked together in the same manner as 65 and 66: despite the conventional numbering, one need not (but may) read them together, just as one need not (but may) read 65 and 66 together. On the controversy, see, e.g., Janan (1994) 174–8; Thomson (1997) 472–4.

[34] Most notably, the "brilliant stream" that "leaps out of a mossy rock" at 68.57–62, which figures either Catullus' flow of tears or the solace offered by Allius (which, one presumes, put an end to the tears); full discussion in Miller (2004) 36–51.

[35] Quinn (1970) 373.     [36] Miller (2004) 31–59; Janan (1994) 112–42.

[37] Quinn (1972) 181.

restlessly in their proper compartments dictated by *alexandrinische Spielerei*.)[38]

Indeed, it may be that the very rigidity of the structure provides cover for material that would otherwise be turned away at the door.

It will take me some time to work my way around to the question of mourning in this poem. An overview is in order.

Catullus begins with an extravagant expression of thanks to one Allius, who, when Catullus was dying of passion (several puzzling similes inserted here), rescued him by lending him a house in which he and his beloved could meet (68.70–2):

> quo mea se molli candida diva pede
> intulit et trito fulgentem in limine plantam
> innixa arguta constituit solea ...

There came my radiant goddess on soft foot, settling the gleaming sole on the worn threshold and pressing down with a creak of her sandal.

Instead of proceeding to a happy recollection of the erotic bliss enjoyed inside this house, Catullus leaves his beloved fixed there on the threshold and swerves into a simile comparing her to the ardent bride Laudamia arriving at the house of her husband, Protesilaus. This simile, itself interrupted and elaborated by a series of further digressions, ends up accounting for fully half of Catullus' poem. First, Catullus supplies an extended narrative of the tragic outcome of Laudamia's passion: Protesilaus was destined to die at Troy, the first casualty of the Trojan War. The mention of Troy then motivates an outburst of grief for Catullus' brother, likewise buried at Troy; as in the letter to Hortalus, the mournful moment is enshrined at the very center of the poem. Working his way back to Laudamia, Catullus illustrates the intensity of her passion with a series of similes bizarre both individually and as a group: the surge of her passion plunged her deeper than the drainage ditch dug by Hercules (an offshoot of the hero's more famous Labors); her rapturous joy in Protesilaus was greater than a grandfather's in the late-born grandson who will inherit his property; and greater too than a wanton dove's pleasure in her mate, the dove who kisses (and now comes

---

[38] Elder (1951) 103.

a triply embedded simile) more unrestrainedly than an especially promiscuous woman. Finally returning to his point of departure, the image
of his beloved joining him at Allius' house, Catullus now acknowledges
a rift in his simile: unlike Protesilaus' Laudamia, his beloved is another
man's wife, and unfaithful to all her men. Yet he resolves, "even though
she is not content with Catullus alone" (*quae tamen etsi uno non est
contenta Catullo*, 135), to endure her infidelities (as Juno puts up with
Jupiter's rovings!) and declares himself content with being her favorite
lover. The poem then closes with a retrospective postscript to Allius
("here's the poem I managed to write for you") and a series of benedic-
tions that begins with Allius and culminates with the beloved, "my light –
while she lives, living is sweet to me" (*lux mea, qua viva vivere dulce mihi
est*, 160).

It is not surprising that the poem, composed as it is of mirror upon
mirror, has generated a whole host of redemptively self-reflexive readings. Micaela Janan argues that the poem celebrates the immortalizing
power of poetry, epitomized by the late-born grandchild, whom she
takes to be "an emblem of Catullus' poetry and its potential to preserve
a representation of the poet after his death." For Janan, even the fluctu-
ating representation of the beloved can be recuperated: "Between a
Lesbia 'not content with Catullus alone' and Lesbia the radiant goddess
stretches the poetic imagination, fired with desire."[39] Others, less sanguine, stabilize the poem by reading it as an allegory of its own difficulties. This strategy was pioneered by Thomas Hubbard, whose 1984 essay
presented the poem as a deconstructive parable, with the house supplied
by Allius standing for the poem and the mistress for the poet's subject
matter; her "trampl[ing]" on the threshold accordingly "implies that the
textual inscription is distorted and problematic, rather than clear-cut."[40]
In an essay written a decade later, Denis Feeney discards the allegorical
specificity but retains the self-reflexive orientation: "the reader's baffled
experience in trying to follow the poet's words becomes a mirror of the
poet's own baffled experience in trying to discover words which will be
adequate."[41] Marilyn Skinner endorses Hubbard's allegorical approach
to the foot on the threshold ("On becoming poetic matter, the mistress
sets her foot down expressively, with a sharp, clear-cut sound. Thus she
limits the text's potential to reach succeeding generations") and reaches

[39] Janan (1994) 135, 140.    [40] Hubbard (1984) 34.    [41] Feeney (1992) 44.

similar conclusions: the poem leaves us "firmly in the grip of paradox, and paradox is the stuff of art ... [Poem 68] convincingly depicts the frustration of the artist still struggling to 'get it right.'"[42] Paul Allen Miller gives Hubbard's reading a Lacanian inflection – "Catullus throughout this poem erects a rigid structure of formal similes, learned literary allusions, and complex ring composition in a homage to the Apollonian forces of the Symbolic only to undermine them through a series of Imaginary identifications" – while adding in a measure of "historical specificity" via the ideologically laden "theme of the house."[43] Yet for Miller too, the labile figuration ultimately counts most insofar as it serves as the vehicle of another simile, with rhetorical slippage supplying a template for ideological slippage, the "double movement of the establishment and violation of the *domus*."[44]

The account I have just provided makes no attempt to do justice to the range and interest of these readings. It is designed only to bring into focus certain tendencies in the criticism recently provoked by this poem. On the one hand, readers are acutely sensitive to its crazy surface. On the other hand, the appeal to self-reflexivity that frames these readings provides too comfortable a solution to the local difficulties they identify and discuss. For all its divergences, Janan's upbeat reading tends likewise to slight the textual surface in favor of the self-reflexive meanings she takes it to bear. She associates Hercules with "productive marriage and immortality," for example.[45] But the couplet on which her description is based (68.115–16) –

> pluribus ut caeli tereretur ianua divis,
> Hebe nec longa virginitate foret

that more gods might wear down the doorway of the sky, and Hebe not be long a virgin –

views Hercules' apotheosis through notably jaundiced eyes (the "wearing down" of the much-visited door suggests promiscuous sexual contacts,

---

[42] Skinner (2003) 157, 172 (with the New Critical "paradox" in place of Hubbard's deconstructive "aporia").

[43] Miller (2004) 48, 52.

[44] Miller (2004) 57; the movement is evident in phrases such as "the same rhetorical shoals" (50), "in the same way" (59), etc.

[45] Janan (1994) 134.

Hebe's marriage appears as negation and curtailment). Nor does it matter to Janan's account of "the logic of successful sexual reproduction"[46] that Hercules enters the poem under cover of a striking periphrasis, as *falsiparens Amphitryoniades*, "the falsely parented son of Amphitryon" (112). The stain of adultery is spreading; the wife has played her husband false, and the name of the father, though it survives and continues to circulate in connection with the son, is deauthenticated in advance.[47] Perhaps this deauthentication serves Hercules' turn, since it is the cuckolding of his mortal father by Jupiter that opens the door to Olympus. But my point is that what Catullus seems to see, when he looks at Hercules, is the product of a sham household: a bastard primed to beget more bastards. The tenor (the "meaning," i.e., apotheosis) may be glorious, but it arrives in a vehicle whose wheels are covered with mud.

In fact the poem generates a whole series of comparable discrepancies. Let us look back at the poem's other "threshold," along with some of what precedes it (68.67–72):

> is clausum lato patefecit limite campum,
>> isque domum nobis isque dedit dominam,[48]
> ad quam communes exerceremus amores.
>> quo mea se molli candida diva pede
> intulit et trito fulgentem in limite plantam
>> innixa arguta constituit solea ...

He [Allius] it was who laid open a closed field by means of a broad path, who gave us a house with its mistress, so that under her roof we might ply our common love. There came my radiant goddess on soft foot, settling the gleaming sole on the worn threshold and pressing down with a creak of her sandal.

As James J. Clauss has pointed out, the imagery of these lines is borrowed from the refined Greek poet whose "Lock of Berenice" Catullus

---

[46] Janan (1994) 134.

[47] The Lacanian ironies swirling around this nonfather's name are fully exploited by Plautus; see Oliensis (2009).

[48] So Thomson (1997) 481, one of many editors to reject the conjectural *dominae* adopted in the OCT.

translated and sent to Hortalus just two poems earlier.[49] Of particular interest here is an epigram in which Callimachus vents his spleen against (in rapid succession) cyclic poetry, the much-traveled path, the promiscuous beloved, the public drinking-well, and all things pertaining to the *demos*. Catullus' "common" love affair, inaugurated upon a "trite" threshold, seems positively designed to invite Callimachean disgust. Every red-blooded Latinist will be tempted to construct on this basis a metapoetic reading of the generic character of Catullus' poem.[50] But if we reverse the direction of interpretation, what the Callimachean subtext can be heard to mutter is that Catullus' beloved is likewise a promiscuous sexual subject, on the move and on the make.

That this "goddess" steps on instead of across the sill surely bodes ill for the union (as readers have recognized, though "Catullus" evidently doesn't).[51] But that is not the only flaw in this fascinating image. This is the moment of maximal idealization: the beloved as the poet's very own "radiant goddess," *mea ... candida diva* (68.70), favoring him with her presence. And yet, like the door to Olympus, the threshold on which she rests her foot is "worn," smoothed by the pressure of innumerable feet, an image that speaks both metonymically and metaphorically of sexual traffic. Much has been written about the metapoetic value of Lesbia's "creaking" sandal (*arguta*, 72; the adjective can also mean "eloquent" or "melodious").[52] But it is worth pointing out that this adjective is also at home in more mundane settings. The only other time Catullus uses a word derived from the root *argut-* is in his racy poem to Flavius, in connection with the telltale "creaking" (*argutatio*, 6.11) of the bed which, "speechless to no avail, proclaims" (*nequiquam tacitum cubile clamat*, 7) the news of Flavius' latest sexual escapade, enjoyed in the company of what Catullus imagines to be "some feverish little whore" (*nescioquid febriculosi / scorti*, 4–5). The smutty rumor circulated by the "creaking sandal," just audible beneath the official laudation of the Laudamia simile, is that the nameless beloved of 68b has at least as much in common with Flavius' anonymous partner as with the renowned heroines of myth. Some might conclude that Catullus is

---

[49] Clauss (1995); the Callimacheanisms extend across more of the passage than I have cited here.

[50] So, with considerable subtlety, Clauss (1995).    [51] See, e.g., Baker (1960).

[52] E.g., Clauss (1995) 244.

ironically (vengefully?) undermining his posture of devotion. Such a conclusion would ascribe the intratextual allusion, as one might then term it, to the author's plan. The ascription could well be correct. But what I have to underscore is that the poem affords no secure basis for an ironic (intentional, rhetorically pointed) reading of moments such as this. The hostile meaning remains latent, pinned in place (and thus localized if not neutralized) by the burden of praise.

The same ambivalence warps the declaration of irrepressible gratitude with which Catullus launches into speech at the start of the poem (68.41–2):

> Non possum reticere, deae, qua me Allius in re
> iuverit aut quantis iuverit officiis.

I can't keep quiet, goddesses, about the matter in which Allius helped me or the great services he did me.

Why, we might ask, should Catullus *not* speak? Read in relation to the cover letter that precedes it, which excuses Catullus' failure to provide the poem his friend Mallius has requested, *non possum reticere* is usually taken to mean something like "even my overwhelming grief can't keep me from celebrating Allius' outstanding benefaction." Read on its own terms, however, the phrase could just as well mean "I can't keep my mouth shut" – as if Catullus were apologizing for an imminent indiscretion, the revelation of a secret or betrayal of a confidence. Again, an instructive parallel is furnished by the poem to Flavius, where Catullus tries to coax a name out of his reticent friend by suggesting that the girl who is keeping him so busy must be embarrassingly uncouth, or Flavius would be not just willing to tell Catullus, but "unable to keep quiet" (*velles dicere nec tacere posses*, 6.3). "Tell me!" Catullus winds up; "I'm longing to summon you, and your love too, up to heaven via a charming piece of verse" (*dic nobis. volo te ac tuos amores / ad caelum lepido vocare versu*, 16–17). Likewise in 68b, Catullus no sooner broaches the topic of Allius' benefaction than he undertakes to broadcast it to the world and posterity (68.45–8):

> sed dicam vobis, vos porro dicite multis
> milibus et facite haec carta loquatur anus
>
> ...
>
> notescatque magis mortuus atque magis ...

39

but I will tell it to you [Muses], and do you in turn tell it to many thousands, and see to it that this page keeps talking when it's an old woman [line missing] so that Allius in death may be better and better known ...

The difference is that the Catullus who addresses Flavius is engaged in a game of urbane dissimulation: his purportedly lofty promise of poetic immortalization wittily reframes a fairly vulgar desire to know, and to disseminate, the latest sexy gossip. Yet the address to Allius is also infected by irony, albeit one not attached to any immediately comprehensible intention on the part of the speaker. The speaker seems bent on praising Allius. But what he has in mind sounds less like immortalization in poetry[53] (after all, Allius appears here as emphatically *mortuus*) than like the operations of a rumor mill, the workings greased by the garrulous "old woman page" of his poetry.[54] Wouldn't the "summons to heaven" Catullus promises Flavius be more appropriate for Allius than this somewhat tawdry image? Contrariwise, wouldn't the *carta anus* be more at home in the poem to Flavius, a fit partner for the talkative bed? The tawdriness is underscored by the proximity of another gabby artifact in poem 67: the chatty, scandal-mongering house door who, despite her prim demeanor, is just waiting to be asked to spill the adulterous secrets of the household she encloses (having survived several previous owners, this door might herself qualify as an "old woman"). Catullus' page will likewise tell a tale of adultery, just as scandalous perhaps, though masquerading as marriage and clad in the fancy dress of myth.

I am suggesting neither that Catullus is "really" threatening to pillory Allius nor that the poem encodes a sneer at his friend's expense, any more than that he is bent on exposing, via touches such as the "creaking sandal," the sins of his mistress. What I am suggesting is that the dirty discourse of gossip is bubbling up through the energetically espoused

---

[53] And Catullus has it backwards – it is supposed to be the poet who is the mediating mouthpiece of the Muses; see Clauss (1995) 240.

[54] On the Hellenistic antecedents of this gossipy figure, see now Hunter (2006) 102. Cf. 78b, where the threatened notoriety is unambiguously negative: *non impune feres; nam te omnia saecla / noscent et, qui sis, fama loquetur anus.*

discourse of praise.[55] As Catullus finally exits the Laudamia simile and returns to his own "bride," the noise begins to form itself into words. After all, his beloved is not *quite* Laudamia's equal (68.131–4):

> Aut nihil aut paulo cui tum concedere digna
> lux mea se nostrum contulit in gremium,
> quam circumcursans hinc illinc saepe Cupido
> fulgebat crocina candidus in tunica.

Either her match or not for below her was my light then, when she conveyed herself into my lap, with Cupid dancing attendance, darting now here and now there, all agleam and radiant in saffron dress.

As in her first appearance at the threshold, so again here the brilliant image is blotted by uncertainty and apprehension.[56] Yet, though Catullus proceeds to acknowledge what his figuration has been darkly communicating all along, the acknowledgment is no sooner made – and made, as if grudgingly, in the form of a concession – than all but canceled (135–7):

> quae tamen etsi uno non est contenta Catullo
> rara verecundae furta feremus erae,
> ne nimium simus stultorum more molesti.

Yet even though she isn't satisfied with Catullus alone, we will put up with the occasional cheating of a modest mistress, for fear of acting like a dolt and being too much of a bore.

That Catullus is working painfully hard to exonerate his beloved is evident in the emphatically thrust-forward palliatives of line 136, *rara verecundae*. Yet if he is shaping himself in the image of the urbanely permissive man of the world, the simile with which he bolsters his

---

[55] An instructive parallel in Thomsen (1992) re the celebratory epithalamic glyconics of poem 61. See, e.g., Thomsen (1992) 74 on the opening line's metrical resemblance (indeed, not just metrical but syllabic or even cryptographic) to the opening of the scurrilous 17 (excoriating an inadequate husband): *Collis o Heliconii | O Colonia, quae cupis*. It is as if the successful marriage fabricated by 61 were haunted by the specter of marital failure.

[56] Cupid is only masquerading as Hymen, and *circumcursans* may conjure up the feckless beloved of the Callimachean epigram.

resolve, as Micaela Janan has pointed out,[57] communicates a residual, doltish rage (138–40):

> saepe etiam Iuno, maxima caelicolum,
> coniugis in culpa flagrantem concoquit iram,
> noscens omnivoli plurima furta Iovis.

even Juno, greatest of heaven's inhabitants, often seethes inwardly with blazing anger at her husband's guilt when she learns of all-desiring Jove's scores of affairs.

Juno may keep her anger banked down, but it burns all the same.

What counts most for me here, though, is not that Catullus is indeed burning but that he persistently disavows, declines to sanction, the emotions to which we might expect him, under the circumstances, to lay claim: rage, disgust, jealousy. These emotions may glimmer through. The question is, why don't they flash out? An instructive contrast is provided by the disenchanted lover of poem 72, self-consciously divided between passion and revulsion: "Now I have come to know you, and so, though I burn the more fiercely, yet I hold you much cheaper and lighter" (*nunc te cognovi: quare etsi impensius uror, | multo mi tamen es vilior et levior*, 5–6).[58] In 68b, however, Catullus not only palliates the sins of his vile mistress but ends by insisting that it is enough for him if she looks forward with special pleasure to the days spent in his company. An "abrupt and disappointing conclusion" indeed,[59] revealing Catullus in a posture of painful abjection, an impression that is not corrected by the subsequent retrospective postscript, with its final extravagant benediction on his wayward mistress, whom he holds not "cheaper" but "dearer" than ever (159–60):

> et longe ante omnes mihi quae me carior ipso est,
> lux mea, qua viva vivere dulce mihi est.

she who far beyond all others is dearer to me than my very self – my light! – while she is alive, living is sweet to me.

---

[57] Janan (1994) 138.

[58] Janan (1994) 140 remarks the contrast only to elide it ("We are again looking at desire as *amo* and *odi* in the conflicting portraits of Lesbia").

[59] Sarkissian (1983) 35; oddly enough, this self-deluding passage is the section of the poem that Hubbard (1984) 35–6 identifies as the moment of deconstructive demystification.

The poem thus ends with the beloved's "light" shining in Catullus' eyes just as blindingly as ever.

Does the author share the blindness of his namesake? In his 1983 monograph on poem 68, John Sarkissian posited a sharp distinction between the self-deluding persona and the omniscient author, who controls every detail of his poem.[60] By contrast Hubbard, just a year after Sarkissian, was already aiming to "transcend the sterile formalism of the New Criticism" via the claim that "[t]he text may rewrite the author's meaning, and the author may not even know his meaning in its full implications."[61] Two decades later, Miller likewise spurns "[p]ersona theory" as "an ideological and rhetorical strategy that allows the critic to continue the New Critical quest for seamless aesthetic unity," finding Hubbard's model "[m]ore satisfying."[62] Hubbard's rejection of authorial omniscience might be expected to produce a liberated (some would say libertine) interpretive practice. And yet it is precisely Sarkissian's New Critical distinction that frees him to produce, as it were with a clear conscience (i.e., without finding fault with Catullus, either as a man or as a poet), his convincingly detailed, all-out demonstration of the lover's perverse determination not-to-know.[63] By contrast, committed as he is to a deconstructive dialectic of blindness and insight, Hubbard is compelled to discover in the poem, however implausibly, "a 'demystified' self which reconsiders experience and feeling through rational deliberation" – deliberation producing, for example, the startling recognition that "marriage is neither desirable nor felicitous."[64] Miller's Catullus is a still more abstract entity, who occupies a "subject position" constituted by "slippages between the normative sexual ideology of the Roman Symbolic (the *matrona* as *verecunda domina* or *era* of a lawfully constituted *domus*); Catullus' Imaginary self-identification (the projection of such values onto his relationship with Lesbia); and the Real (the impossibility of these two realms ever coinciding)."[65] This is persuasive, but does little more than reformulate something we may feel we, and Catullus too, already knew: that Catullus

---

[60] Sarkissian (1983) 1–4, 39–41.　　[61] Hubbard (1984) 29, 30.　　[62] Miller (2004) 51.

[63] A project launched in the final lines of Catullus' most famous poem, with the lover proposing to scramble the erotic accounts, not only to ward off the knowledge of others, but to prevent "our knowing," *ne sciamus*, 5.11.

[64] Hubbard (1984) 43, 37. In effect, Sarkissian identifies a similarly "demystified" self (the author) but locates it outside the poem.

[65] Miller (2004) 56.

dreams (= the Imaginary) of setting up house with Lesbia in proper, marital style (= the Symbolic), but can't (= the Real).[66]

Meanwhile the problem of intention is left in abeyance.[67] This may be – it often is – just where it belongs. Still, reading can often profit from thinking about intentions, especially insofar as they are, or are made to seem, mislaid or derailed. The mournful labor of Orpheus is more interesting because Orpheus doesn't mean to mourn and doesn't know that he is mourning. The apple simile at the end of 65 means more insofar as its guilty meaning takes its author by surprise. Thus I share Sarkissian's pre-postmodern interest in the quasi-dramatic character-ization of the dazzled speaker while also believing, in company with Hubbard and Miller, that the author is not master in his own house, or at least that his mastery is never undisputed or absolute. Psychoanalysis (like deconstruction) is not only a set of meanings but a theory of reading, hospitable to the "close reading" of New Criticism,[68] while providing a less constricted view of what counts for interpretation – less constricted, for example, than Sarkissian's, which can see the author's knowledge and the speaker's blindness, but not the twilit area in between.

In a famous epigram, Catullus diagnoses his own excruciating con-dition as an inexplicable crossing of love and hate: *odi et amo* (85.1). What produces the textual unconscious of 68b, I am suggesting, is in part the repression of the *odi*. Unlike the self-aware epigram, this poem does not express but sporadically vents its ambivalence, in "unauthor-ized" formulations – the gossipy page, the hyper-experienced thresh-old, the creaking sandal. A limit case perhaps is provided by the punning appearance of the antithesis *eros/eris* across two neighboring couplets:

---

[66] Likewise Miller (2004) 59: "the *domus* theme and its slippages reveal a longing [ = the Imaginary] for a lawful household with a lawful *domina* [ = the Symbolic] that Catullus cannot acquire [ = the Real]."

[67] When Miller (2004) 58 remarks an "irony" "not to be lost" in Cupid's masquerad-ing as Hymen, are we to imagine Catullus controlling the irony, or is he the one, the only one perhaps, on whom it is lost?

[68] And of course deconstruction was attacked from early on as nothing more than a new New Criticism: similarly ahistorical, decontextualized, etc.

... hostia caelestis pacificasset **eros**. (68.76)
([before] a sacrifice had placated the heavenly masters)
... quod temere invitis suscipiatur **eris**. (68.78)
(whatever is rashly undertaken against the will of the masters)

Did Catullus intend this ungrammatical bilingual pun? Possibly. If he didn't, can it be said to be "there" at all? Yes – before my eyes, in my ears. Could it be that the pun, even if Catullus didn't know it, helped him settle on this polyptoton? Perhaps he liked the shape of these couplets both because the pun was there and because he didn't (quite) know it. In John Shoptaw's terms, the antithesis is not a pun (pointed, witty, intended) but a cryptographic formation, which Catullus may not have meant, but which he effectively sanctioned via what Shoptaw identifies as the fundamental "textual act," the authorial *stet*, which sets the text via a definitive "let it stand."[69]

If I were to produce a self-reflexive reading of 68b, I would read it not as a fable of blocked communication but as a complement to the mannerist experiment of poem 64. There Catullus folds the story of the abandoned Ariadne into an account of the wedding of Peleus and Thetis. From the image of Ariadne woven into the coverlet that drapes the marriage bed, pictured gazing from the shore after Theseus' departing ship, the narrator spins out the whole story (Theseus' arrival in Crete, her falling in love, the death of the Minotaur, her abandonment, her curse on Theseus and its fulfillment), including a lengthy sample of the kind of soliloquy, progressing from grief to rage, that she was wont to perform in those unhappy days. The irony of inserting such a tragic tale of love gone bad into the happy wedding scene is obvious enough. But when we scrutinize the coverlet as the narrator enables us to reconstruct it (i.e., the imagined artifact to which the description is so tenuously attached), we find that what it displays is not just Ariadne abandoned, gazing with mournful eyes after the departing Theseus, but Ariadne on the verge of a union with the god Bacchus, who is heading her way "from another part" (*at parte ex alia*, 64.251) of the coverlet, accompanied by his noisy, rejoicing retinue.[70] Whereas the design of the coverlet seems to depict

---

[69] Shoptaw (2000) 224.

[70] Such a reconstruction is legitimate and even solicited by the poem, which is exploring, in good ecphrastic style, the differences between its representing and

Ariadne and Dionysus (a wedding in the making), the poet who describes it is evidently preoccupied by what it does not represent – the sad affair of Ariadne and Theseus.[71] It is as if the poem were the work of a narrator so melancholy that he could not but distort the image before him ("paint it black," as it were). On the other hand, in the framing narrative of the wedding of Peleus and Thetis, the narrator takes the opposite tack, repeatedly insisting on the couple's happiness, when "everyone knows" that the union was foisted upon a furiously reluctant Thetis and did not last long. That the narrator is not just adopting a happier variant of this famous myth is clear from the notoriously perverse culmination of the wedding song he entrusts to the Fates, who, after foretelling the early death of the couple's murderous son Achilles and the ghastly sacrifice of the virgin Polyxena at his tomb, proceed blithely to exhort the happy couple, and on that bloody basis (*quare agite*, 372), to join together in longed-for love. The net result of the combination of the two accounts is to display the distorting effects of narrative intervention, caught in the very act of making black white and white black.[72] Poem 68b is another such experiment, a transparent attempt at whitewashing the faithless mistress into a "radiant goddess." But the shift from the third-person hexameters of 64 to the first-person elegiac couplets of 68b, featuring as they do a character named Catullus with a dead brother buried at Troy, means that we can't draw a clean line (even if we wanted to) between the mannerist distortion and the psychic investment that helps produce it.[73]

## About the brother: the dirt of Troy

To this point, my reading has slighted the brother in favor of the mistress. For most of its 120 lines, the poem displays the same bias. Unlike 65

represented media. It is possible that the poet's narration of (e.g.) Theseus killing the Minotaur and Aegeus killing himself is inspired by other scenes on the tapestry, ones he has not chosen to identify as such (i.e., he includes no representational "flags" such as *ex parte alia, describitur*, etc.). But the poem is explicitly attached to the artifact only at the beginning and the ending: Ariadne by the shore, Bacchus approaching. See Gaisser (1995) 600, 607.

[71] So Forsyth (1980) 101.

[72] Similarly (but more subtly) Schmale (2004) 219–20.

[73] Of course, 64 is already a magnet for psychologizing readings, e.g., Putnam (1982) 49–60 on Catullus' identification with the abandoned Ariadne.

(and also unlike 68a, the cover letter attached to 68b, as 65 to 66), 68b is not framed by professions of disabling grief; Catullus appears preoccupied with his debt to the living, his benefactor Allius, not the dead. Yet the dead brother will succeed all the same in extorting an interim payment from the forgetful survivor. Catullus' gratitude to Allius is backed up by a happy reminiscence of the tryst Allius' benefaction made possible. But this reminiscence is no sooner launched than hijacked by the figure of Laudamia. And though Laudamia finds her way into the poem as an image of the beloved, it has been clear to many readers that the choice falls upon this particular heroine – so unsuitable, after all, in so many ways, as a figure for Catullus' errant mistress – because she is the very embodiment of mourning, no sooner gaining than losing her husband to the Trojan expedition in which he was fated to die.[74] The unlikely simile that identifies the beloved with Laudamia seems partly, even essentially, determined by Catullus' own unconfessed, as it were "unauthorized," identification with Laudamia.

It is the mention of Troy that triggers, as if spontaneously, via an accidental metonymical convergence, the memory of the dead brother who lies buried there, along with so many others (68.87–92):

> nam tum Helenae raptu primores Argivorum
>   coeperat ad sese Troia ciere viros,
> Troia (nefas!) commune sepulcrum Asiae Europaeque,
>   Troia virum et virtutum omnium acerba cinis,
> quaene etiam nostro letum miserabile fratri
>   attulit. ei misero frater adempte mihi ...

For at that time [of Laudamia's marriage] Troy through the rape of Helen had begun to summon the Argive chieftains to her side; Troy (unspeakable horror!) the common grave of Asia and Europe, Troy the untimely ash of all heroes and heroic deeds, [Troy] who brought wretched death upon my brother too. Alas, brother taken from me, leaving me wretched ...

Catullus closes off his fraternal digression by underscoring the hateful distance of the alien grave site, which keeps the brother from being ritually reintegrated into his community (97–101):

---

[74] E.g., Janan (1994) 121–2.

> quem nunc tam longe non inter nota sepulcra
> > nec prope cognatos compositum cineres
> sed Troia obscena, Troia infelice sepultum
> > detinet extremo terra aliena solo.
> ad quam tum properans ...

[you brother] whom now, so far away, not among familiar graves, nor laid to rest near kindred ashes, an alien land holds fast, buried in obscene Troy, ill-omened Troy, in remotest earth. To that land then hastening [came the Greek army ...]

No doubt Catullus has designed the poem, as he designed 65, so as to produce an occasion for this central, mournful divagation; the effect of spontaneity is carefully calculated, and the "accidental" metonymy is itself an authorial device. On the other hand, the simile that lets Catullus perform his endless grief also jeopardizes the success of the performance. Laudamia is famous because she could not forget her husband – her devotion knew no bounds. After losing Protesilaus, she clung to his image (whether a statue fashioned in his likeness, or his ghost, dispatched for a final rendezvous by the pitying gods),[75] and upon losing the image, she killed herself. Certainly 68b is a poem obsessed with, even insatiable for, images.[76] Unlike Laudamia, however, Catullus does not remain true to his lost brother, but sets up images of others (Allius, himself, his mistress) in his brother's place. The mourner may lament the "pleasant light taken from a wretched brother" (*misero fratri iucundum lumen ademptum*, 93) and assert that "all" the "joys" once nurtured by his live brother's "sweet love" (*quae tuus in vita dulcis alebat amor*, 96) lie buried in the grave with him, but the lover identifies "light" and the "sweetness" of life with the person of his living mistress (*lux mea, qua viva vivere dulce mihi est*, 160). Troy not only makes Catullus remember his brother, it may also be what encourages him guiltily to forget, as if the brother, so far out of sight, were also out of mind. If Catullus cannot fault his fickle mistress, cannot find her guilty, one reason is that he too is an unfaithful lover, who has put it in his brother's power, if the dead could speak, to level a disillusioned *dicebas quondam* against the man who once said "I will love you forever" (*semper amabo*, 65.11).

---

[75] On the equivalence, Bettini (1999) 11–12.

[76] *imago* encompasses statue, ghost, and simile (as well as indexical death-mask); cf. less capacious terms such as *simile, similitudo, simulacrum*.

Once again we are reminded that for the mourner, forgetting is murder. When the Laudamia simile carries his poem off to Troy, what Catullus remembers, along with his dead brother, is the Trojan playboy whose pleasures the Greek army leaves home to interrupt: "to keep Paris from enjoying his stolen adulteress and passing his time in unhindered ease in a tranquil bedroom" (*ne Paris abducta gavisus libera moecha / otia pacato degeret in thalamo*, 68.103–4). The immediate point is the contrast with Laudamia, deprived of marital bliss (*coniugium*, 107) in consequence of Paris' adultery. But the legendary lovers also hold up a mirror to Catullus and the mistress who (we soon discover) is likewise the property of another man.[77] It is as if their sexual pleasure were not just the forgetting but the very cause of the brother's death. In the previous section I argued that the dirty muttering audible across the poem fingers the unacknowledged promiscuity of the mistress. Could it be that what motivates this muttering is not (only) her guilt but his, the same blood guilt that spilled out of the similes of 65? In the translation accompanying 65, the recently stellified lock of Berenice remembers how the newlywed queen wept and wailed when her husband set off for war (the poem is a consequence of the vow she then took, to offer a lock of her hair upon his safe return). It is with urbane skepticism that the lock records the queen's attempts (exploiting the pharaonic language of brother–sister marriage) to dissimulate the sexual desire that fueled those desperate tears: "so it wasn't your being abandoned in an empty bed that you were mourning, but the heartrending separation from a dear brother?" (*et tu non orbum luxti deserta cubile, / sed fratris cari flebile discidium?*, 66.21–2).[78] One might harbor the same doubts in regard to the protestations of 68b. Is Catullus mourning an erotic or a fraternal loss? Or have the two somehow gotten so tangled up with each other as to be no longer readily distinguishable?

Tears are indeed abundantly shed in poem 68b, but for what, or for whom? The confusion is written into the famously elusive simile that

---

[77] See, e.g., Miller (2004) 54: "Catullus directly associates the death of his brother with his own adulterous behavior." For my reading, it matters that the association is *not* direct; nowhere explicitly avowed, Catullus' guilt seeps out of the myth.

[78] For many readers (e.g., Thomson (1997) 448), the biographical resonance of this couplet helps explain Catullus' choice of this particular poem to translate.

rounds off Catullus' opening address to the Muses. Those goddesses know (*scitis*, 68.52), he insists, the desperate plight from which Allius rescued him, when he was burning with passion and flooded with tears (55–60):

> maesta neque assiduo tabescere lumina fletu
>     cessarent tristique imbre madere genae.
> qualis in aerii perlucens vertice montis
>     rivus muscoso prosilit e lapide,
> qui cum de prona praeceps est valle volutus,
>     per medium densi transit iter populi ...

[when] my sorrowful eyes were ceaselessly worn down by constant weeping, my cheeks drenched by sad showers. Like a pellucid stream atop a high mountain which leaps from a mossy rock-face, and after rolling headlong down a slanting valley passes right through a path thronged with people ...

The clear mountain stream illustrates, so one initially supposes, the gush of Catullus' hot tears. But the sense seems to shift as the passage proceeds. The simile is followed (or doubled?) by another, this one explicitly linked to the saving intervention of Allius: like the favoring breeze that answers the prayers of a tempest-tossed sailor, "such a source of aid was Allius to me" (*tale fuit nobis Allius auxilium*, 66). Perhaps, then, the refreshing stream should likewise be linked, not with Catullus' distress, but with its alleviation? should be taken, that is, with what follows it instead of with what precedes? Paul Allen Miller has concluded that the attempt to settle the issue (and there are excellent arguments to be made on either side) is not just hopeless but misguided, the confusion of "cause and effect, subject and object, anxiety and aid" being, in his view, precisely the point.[79] I agree with Miller, and I have no interest in reopening the question. But what intrigues me about the simile is less its undecidability than its interactions with another simile, likewise the burden of seemingly incompatible meanings: the "apple" simile from the end of the letter to Hortalus.[80] The interaction is superficial,

---

[79] Miller (2004) 50.
[80] The resemblance of the problems posed by these similes has been discussed, but not (so far as I am aware) the mutual interference of their diction.

involving the sound more than the sense, which may be why it has passed unremarked:

> rivus muscoso **prosilit** e lapide,
> qui cum de **prona praeceps** est valle volutus (68.58–9)
>     dum adventu matris **prosilit**, excutitur,
> atque illud **prono praeceps** agitur decursu (65.22–3)

Perhaps *prosilit* brought *prona praeceps* in its train, as the merest quasi-automatic echo of a turn of phrase Catullus had invented in 65 (the poetic chronology can, of course, be inverted without damage to the argument). Yet once the similes are brought into relation, other motives for their conjunction emerge. In the opening line of 65, Catullus represented himself as crushed by constant grief, *assiduo … dolore*, over his brother's death; in the final line, he leaves us with the image of the maiden with a blush spreading over her "sad face," *tristi … ore* (24). The maiden is sad because she is distressed, discomposed. But she is also sad, at another level, because she carries the poet's grief for his brother. The grief recounted in the comparable lines of 68b is, by all accounts, entirely erotic: the "constant weeping" and "sad showers" that flooded Catullus before Allius intervened are evidence of an affliction sent by Venus (*Amathusia*, 51). Yet the recounting of these tears seems to trigger a memory of those other tears, the ones shed for the dead brother. It is as if the very superabundance of weeping flagged the displacement of one grief by another. There may also be something to learn from *prosilit*, a verb for which Catullus finds use only in these two passages. The verb looks a bit like a punning explication of the name of **Prot**esil**a**us, the doomed hero who was the "first" to "leap forth" onto the shore of Troy. I begin to wonder whether the maiden who "leaps up" has already incorporated something of Protesilaus within herself, along with the lost apple.

As in the letter to Hortalus, the most persuasive performances of grief are to be found not in the central apostrophe for which the author has so carefully set the stage, but in passages shaped by mournful pressures of which the poet seems quite unaware. Invective against the grave site is a conventional feature of elegy, it is true. But the vehemence of Catullus' anaphoric assault on Troy seems disproportionate, even so. It is as if we were witnessing the effects of a displacement, with Troy attracting all the rage and horror Catullus is fending off from his guilty self and cannot vent against his wanton beloved. Troy is, indeed, the greatest, perhaps the only true villain of this poem. It is Troy, conveniently feminine in gender, who entices men to their doom (*ad sese Troia ciere viros*, 68.88);[81] Troy, the "common grave" (*commune sepulcrum*, 89), who promiscuously embraces vast contingents of men;[82] Troy who is *obscena* (99), not just "ill-omened" but, less abstractly, with her alien "earth" and distant "soil" (*extremo terra aliena solo*, 100), "filthy" or even just plain "obscene."[83] As for the lovers plying their "common love" in a borrowed house: *they* find their composite image not in the Trojan grave site – certainly not! – but in Laudamia, passionate mistress and mindful mourner. Yet as I have tried to show, the dirt on the mistress is not just hard to scrape off, it is constantly being laid on even thicker by the very figurative instruments that are called upon to remove it. Catullus' inability *in this poem* to articulate the ambivalence he so readily voices elsewhere is the result of a kind of fraternal interference, not only because condemning the faithlessness of his mistress would mean confronting his own, but also because acknowledging her promiscuity would be to discover in himself, buried in his soiled mistress, the very image of his dead brother. His insistent idealization of her as the "light" is a way of escaping the all-embracing tomb.

There is, of course, another, simpler explanation. The poem is an elaborate thank-you note to Allius; and one does not fault a gift in the act of gratefully acknowledging it. To erupt in mourning for a brother in whose death Allius had no part is one thing. To fulminate against the very woman whose favors Allius enabled Catullus to enjoy would be quite another. Decorum, social and rhetorical, may indeed contribute its share to the repression of the Catullan *odi* here. And yet the thank-you note is itself caught up in the unhappy labor of inadequate mourning. It is true that the opening praise of Allius bears no obvious traces of the grief that will erupt at the center of the poem; it is as if Catullus had quite

---

[81] Janan (1994) 130 aptly entitles her discussion of this section "Siren Troy."

[82] Elsewhere (11.18–20) Catullus accuses Lesbia of embracing "three hundred lovers at a time" and "breaking the groin of each and every one"; "groin" = *ilia*, which cryptographically supports the genital identity of Troy/Ilium in 68b.

[83] The language of the sewer recurs in the drainage pit dug by Hercules in the very "marrows" of a mountain, the pit that drains the marsh and dries the rich soil; like Troy, the *barathrum* is an underworldly space with corporeal (potentially obscene) implications.

forgotten his dead brother, or had at least set that memory aside until the appointed hour of its resurgence, some forty lines later. Still, there is something disquieting about this passage. Catullus cannot fail to speak about Allius and his good deed, he announces, "lest fugitive time with its forgetful centuries cover up these exertions of his with black night" (*ne fugiens saeclis obliviscentibus aetas / illius hoc caeca nocte tegat studium*, 68.43–4). And the Muses must amplify his commemoration so as to prevent Allius' ever being forgotten (48–50):

> notescatque magis mortuus atque magis
> nec tenuem texens sublimis aranea telam
> in deserto Alli nomine opus faciat.

so that, in death, he may come to be more and more renowned, and no spider, weaving delicate webs on high, produce its work over Allius' neglected name.

True and interesting things have been written about this passage (about the Callimachean spider weaving its programmatically delicate web, for example).[84] But what I want to underscore is just the redundancy, the disproportionate emphasis, of Catullus' rhetoric here. An expression of gratitude is normally keyed to three factors: the significance of the favor granted, the degree of intimacy between grantor and grantee, and their relative status.[85] But none of these quite accounts for this Catullan effusion.[86] Indeed, everything takes place as if the passage were fueled by an energy that has been diverted from its original object, one whose identity is not far to seek. The insistent imagining of Allius dead (*mortuus* is an unnecessary specification, after all) joins with the fantasy of the web-shrouded name, incised upon some forgotten tombstone, to point toward the other man, the really dead man, that Catullus is not only forgetting but unwittingly, and therefore all the more energetically, remembering as he composes these lines for Allius.[87]

---

[84] Clauss (1995) 240–2.

[85] This is basic politeness theory; see, e.g., Brown and Levinson (1987).

[86] Cf. Catullus' thank-you note to Cicero, where it is our ignorance regarding Cicero's benefaction (trivial or earth-shaking? or merely a fictional premise enabling this ambiguous performance?) that produces the famous indeterminacy of the tone.

[87] The meaning of Catullus' desire to keep Allius *notus* and his tombstone tended comes into focus when he laments the brother buried *non inter nota sepulcra* (68.97).

The same wayward energy may help determine the form of the address to Allius at the other end of the poem (68.149–50):

> Hoc tibi, quod potui, confectum carmine munus
> pro multis, Alli, redditur officiis ...

This tribute accomplished in poetry, all I could manage, is rendered to you, Allius, in return for many services ...

These "services" are those about which Catullus proved incapable of remaining silent at the start of the poem (*quantis ... officiis*, 42); the repetition signals that the end of the poem is approaching. But the closing renewal of thanks, like the opening sequence, also communicates, *sotto voce*, the tribute to the brother that it has supplanted. Substitute *frater* for *Alli*, and the couplet becomes a suitable postscript to poem 101, the famous elegy (itself a *confectum carmine munus*; cf. *munere* at 101.3, 8) that represents Catullus faithfully performing the final rites at his brother's Trojan grave site, and that ends with his last "hail and farewell":

> *Hoc tibi, quod potui, confectum carmine munus
> pro multis, frater, redditur officiis.

In effect: "this funeral offering accomplished in poetry, all I could manage, is rendered to you, brother," not in return for but "in place of the many services," the ongoing dutiful observances, that Catullus will not be able to render his dead brother, buried as he is so far from home. This is not the couplet Catullus wrote, but its suppression shapes the one he did.

## Three preliminary conclusions

(1) Readings that listen for the textual unconscious are fragmentary, necessarily and even programmatically so. Though much may be gained from thinking about Orpheus' song as an unwitting elegy for Eurydice, such a reading cannot account for the whole of Orpheus' performance, or even for the whole of any one episode within it. The ghost of Eurydice resurfaces here and there (most obviously in Pygmalion's ivory statue, most flittingly in fleet Atalanta), but for long stretches of Orpheus' song she seems content to remain quietly underground. Likewise, the

girl with the "sad face" may express the grieving Catullus, but that does not mean that we should extend the identification back across the simile and incorporate the fiancé and mother into the mournful scenario. Indeed, if Eurydice's outline were discernible throughout Orpheus' song, if Catullus' grief marked the apple simile from start to finish, one would have to do not with the textual unconscious, but with something more properly termed a poetic theme or a pattern of imagery. The textual unconscious is detected, or comes into being, in its irruptions; there has to be a normative textuality in place, if only to provide the fictitious occasion for the irruption.

(2) What I am calling normative textuality is defined (loosely, roughly) by syntax, word order, and various other structures that cue readerly understanding (it is always possible to argue about these cues, of course, but not always – Catullus 68b is a glaring exception – necessary or particularly interesting). One reason my discussion focuses so often on similes is that this device seems designed to enable a dialogue between the normative text (the official point of comparison, flagged by *ut, qualis*, etc.) and the wayward meanings that crash the poem under cover of the authorized comparison. It is because I am interested in this textual dynamics, this texture, that I put so much stress on hierarchies of meaning. This is why I insist, for example, on the narrator's insistence that Orpheus is *by no means* guilty nor even, by the time he launches into his great performance, *mindful* of his wife's death. It does not follow, of course, that we cannot read Orpheus as, precisely, both guilty and mindful. To the contrary, it is just the discrepancy between the claims of the teller and the logic of the tale that gives such a reading its full value. It is just insofar as Orpheus mourns *even so*, and *despite everything*, that the song functions as the simulacrum of an authentic event of mourning. If we let go of the surface organization, we give up the possibility of distinguishing what is said from what is communicated.

(3) These readings lay emphasis on effects that are meaningful not because they are intended, but because they are not. What would it mean to claim that Catullus "intended" Allius to stand in for his brother? Such an intention strikes me at least as unintelligible, i.e., I see no way to feed it back into interpretation. A philological fundamentalist might reply that the relation between Allius and the brother must then be a chimera, the product of my fevered imagination; an intertextual fundamentalist might retort, to the contrary, that the relation is "there" and available because

the poem participates in a discursive universe in which one direct address (say) can always potentially bring into play any or indeed every other. Yet I still want to develop an interpretation of the dynamic of *this particular* relationship. What then? If I proceed to say that Catullus did *not* intend Allius to stand in for his brother, that the relation "happened" *despite* his intentions, that it even distorted his poem by producing a disproportionate gush of gratitude to Allius, I leave myself open to accusations of hubris (how can I pretend to understand Catullus' poem better than Catullus himself does?). I can sidestep the accusation by claiming that after all Catullus did intend this effect: that it was Catullus who designed the disproportion to register the presence of the hovering brother. But though it is always possible to reestablish an authorial intention on the other side of the textual mirror, this conventional solution is itself predicated on a narcissistic projection – as if the author's meaning answered exactly to the critic's understanding! This does not mean I will refrain from ascribing intentions to my authors (and believing my ascriptions), only that I do not always consider it necessary or useful to anchor the textual unconscious in the author's intention. Indeed, if intention were all, reading would be but a poor and pleasureless endeavor. All interpretation, conventional and newfangled alike, is begotten in the blank spaces of not-knowing, both within and between the writer and the reader.

# Murdering mothers

When it came to mothers, as Nicole Loraux has remarked, the oedipally minded Freud had his own blind spot.[1] The relation of mother to son appeared to Freud as the least fraught of human associations. The mother might cherish the son whose arrival supplied her want of a penis, and the son might take the mother as his first object of desire, one never entirely abandoned, but these fond emotions are relatively unproblematic; it is the intrusion of the father that makes the really interesting difference. It would be left to Melanie Klein and others working with the very young to uncover the exciting world of infantile fantasy, in which the mother, or the mother's breast, internalized in both "good" and "bad" forms, plays so signal a role, most notoriously negative: devoured and devouring, eviscerated and eviscerating. Whereas the Freudian father provides (if not in his own person, then in the function he more or less successfully represents) the structure and telos of action, this mother is simply *embarrassing*: she is what the reader and the hero are normally hastening to get past. This chapter is my attempt to slow down and bring the mother into better focus.

If psychoanalysts of Roman literature and culture have tended to pay more attention to the father, it is out of deference not just to the Freudian bias but to the overwhelmingly paternal cast of Roman ideology. After all, the Roman father appears to be a truly formidable figure.

---

[1] Loraux (1998) 51 ("Blindness on the part of the inventor of 'Oedipus'?"); on Freud's occluded mother, see further Sprengnether (1990). When Freud touches on "the surprising, yet regular, fear of being killed (?devoured) by the mother" (Freud (1931) 227), it is a daughter's fear he means, not a son's.

The all-powerful head of his household, he is endowed (we are told) even with the "right of life and death" (*ius vitae necisque*): the right to sell his children, even to kill them, not only as infants (when many a child will have been exposed) but, much more shockingly, as adults. The father's supremacy is also registered in the Roman system of nomenclature, which disseminates the father's name to his offspring and also to his freedmen and freedwomen. Marcus Tullius Cicero, for example, had a daughter named Tullia, a son named Marcus Tullius Cicero, and a slave who would be known, once freed, as Marcus Tullius Tiro. Of course, like most "last names" today, the name was not Cicero's "own" but came to him from his own father, who got it from his; the number of Tullii Cicerones is in principle unlimited. The results can be very confusing for students of Roman culture, and must have been confusing also for Romans trying to negotiate their own history, in which the identical names kept recurring. But identity seems to be precisely the point. In the ideal scenario, the son reproduces a father who reproduces his father, and so on across the generations. As the medium of the father's reproduction in his son, the mother performs best when she shows least. *Pudicitia* is a negative virtue, the absence of distorting interference in the family line: Catullus' Iunia, for example, will prove her chastity by producing a son who looks just like his father (Catull. 61.214–18).

Roman domestic and legal practices also help drain the mother of psychoanalytic interest. As recent work on the family has underscored, the Roman mother was not an especially "motherly" figure.[2] Though cropping up occasionally, the image of the doting mother (counterweight to the severe father) does not have the status of a stereotype; in general, mother and father were not so sharply distinguished. In the elite family, the mother kept her distance from the nursery, leaving the tasks of handling, bathing, and nursing infants to slaves, with the wet-nurse playing an especially important role. And when she did enter her child's life, it was in company with the father, and in a similar role, as educator, adviser, etc. This relative distance was reinforced by the mother's legal standing. At least from the late Republic on, a wife usually remained, for the purposes of property rights and inheritance, in the family of her father, whose name she continued to bear, and it was normally the husband who kept charge of the children in the event of a divorce.

---

[2] E.g., Dixon (1988), on whom this paragraph draws heavily.

How could, why would, a Roman boy come to desire a mother so distant and disembodied? What becomes of that crucial psychic object, the mother's breast, if the son has never encountered it? As Marilyn Skinner has argued, the "[s]exual subjectivity" produced in such a setting might well be expected to diverge from "any form of subjectivity produced in the present-day nuclear family."[3] Roman subjectivity would then be impervious to the theories Freud and his successors developed around that nucleus.

Of course, such a historically specific account impugns the omnipotent father along with the nurturing mother. In truth, Roman fathers were not local gods, and their powers were constrained and limited from all sides – by the claims of wives, the demands of children, custom, peer pressure, etc. Moreover, as Brent Shaw has demonstrated, there is no evidence that any Roman father ever had, much less exercised, the legal authority, in his capacity as father (as opposed to military commander, say), to kill his child; the much touted "right of life and death" is a chimera. On the other hand, as Shaw points out, it is to the Romans that we owe this myth; it is their myth, not (just) ours.[4] What Suzanne Dixon's study of the Roman mother likewise shows is not only that most elite women did not nurse their children but also that the ideal of the nursing mother persisted all the same.[5] Again, judging from Keith Bradley's studies of the Roman household, one might expect a proliferation of stories about nurses, tutors, and other members of the extended family.[6] Such characters do play a part, especially in the "lower" genres of comedy, satire, and epigram (always more hospitable to the "lower" orders of society). Yet when it comes to picturing the family, Roman literature tends to slight the servile caretakers in favor of a streamlined grouping featuring the conventional trio of father, mother, and baby. Focusing attention on the overlooked extended *familia* has proven to be

[3] Skinner (1997) 133; in the event, Skinner's counter-model (founded on the myth of the Great Mother) replaces the Freudian Oedipus with the "omnipotent mother" dear to object-relations theory. See, e.g., Chasseguet-Smirgel (1970) 112–19; Benjamin (1995) (with a critical review of the concept).

[4] Shaw (2001).

[5] "[T]he only certain statements we can make about wet-nursing in wealthy circles in Rome are that it was the norm ... and that it was routinely denounced" (Dixon [1988] 120).

[6] Bradley (1991) (with a discussion of the *nutrix* at 13–36).

one of the most fruitful directions in contemporary Roman studies. But what counts for me here is that Freud is in good Roman company in misrepresenting (in Skinner's words) "the actual circumstances of Roman family life."[7]

The historicist critique of psychoanalysis tends to operate with a very reduced model of causation. What *is* the relation between individual or national history and subjectivity? How *do* people come about? Causal explanations are liable to turn in one's hands; the interposition of the wet-nurse, for example, far from preventing infantile ambivalence toward the mother's breast, might be taken to register the persistence of that ambivalence in the parents who employ her.[8] Though his work often posits events as triggers, Freud also acknowledged the gap between recurring psychic structures and particular biographical events. It was the mystery of how the oedipal situation kept (as he thought) recurring that Freud was trying to address via the myth of the primal horde and the hypothesis of inherited memory. Lacan's solution, the one Latinists have generally found most congenial, was a radical abstraction, whereby the individual mother and father are replaced by their roles in the psychic orders of the Imaginary and the Symbolic, roles that predate and outlast the actual parents and that need not be inhabited by them. Without embracing either solution, one may yet recognize that both writers are confronting a significant challenge.

If the psyche is not simply or straightforwardly the product of its circumstances, no more is art simply or straightforwardly the product of the psyche. Yet some relationship, however hard to track, there surely is. High Roman literature may not accurately reflect elite domestic practices (or "reality") but may still be an index of another reality. Indeed, the stylizations of genre, convention, and virtuoso poetic technique may license fantasy just to the degree that they supersede realism (this is in nuce Erich Segal's argument re Plautus' "Greek" comedy).[9] Be that as it may, I am not delving into my texts to expose the dark

---

[7] Skinner (1997) 133.

[8] Indeed, as Janet Adelman argues re Shakespeare's England, wet-nursing may actually have intensified the "hold of the mother on the imagination" by giving "the child two psychic sites of intense maternal deprivation rather than one"; see Adelman (1992) 5.

[9] "The Roman superego is satisfied by the Greek masquerade, and the audience enjoys an inward revel" (Segal (1987) 41).

secrets of anyone's psyche. I am interested in the unconscious not for itself but for the seductive fissuring that it produces at the textual surface. At the formalist extreme, this unconscious may be considered as a content-indifferent mechanism of textual production, a Riffaterrean hypogram in psychoanalytic dress: *something* (and it doesn't really matter what) needs to be repressed so that textuality can flower over its grave. Still, as the preceding paragraphs will suggest, though remaining agnostic about the ultimate truth value of the fables of psychoanalysis, I am not prepared to give up on their specially charged status, even if this status is in truth only the secondary effect of an ideological demand (one can always delve deeper … ).

For Virgil and Ovid, motherhood is poetically productive just to the degree that it is problematic, and in quite a classic psychoanalytic sense. The stories they repress can be assimilated to the myths of psychoanalysis: a Kleinian fable of the son's fantastic fears (Virgil), a Freudian divagation on the mother's desire (Ovid). Yet I am also interested in tracking their lateral engagement with other discourses that revolve the mysterious question of origins. For my reading of Virgil, the origins at issue are literary; for my reading of Ovid, they are Roman and political.

## The danger of the mother in Virgil's *Aeneid*

If any hero could be forgiven for harboring incestuous yearnings, it is surely Aeneas, the son of no less a personage than Venus, the divine incarnation of sexual desire. As if to sidestep the issue, Virgil generally keeps the mother away from her son. Not for this pair the affectionate intimacy that binds the Homeric Thetis and Achilles. In their first interview, Venus does not come close to Aeneas and "stroke him with her hand" (the gesture of Thetis at *Iliad* 1.361). Instead, she addresses him from afar, disguised as a mortal huntress, so that Aeneas mistakes her for her virginal antithesis, "Apollo's sister, or one of her nymphs" (*Aen.* 1.329).[10] Venus thus acts as her son's helper (filling him in on local conditions, bolstering his spirits with an encouraging prophecy) while leaving the maternal role effectively vacant. The scene is notoriously

---

[10] This moment opens onto another incestuous scenario, one fostered by the agelessness of the goddess. On the incestuous pairing of Dido-Diana and Aeneas-Apollo (previewed in Venus' choice of disguise), see Schiesaro (2005) 96–7; Hardie (2006).

overdetermined by multiple intertexts – Venus-as-Diana incorporates the competing goddesses of Euripides' *Hippolytus* as well as features of the Odyssean Athena and Nausicaa, all the while preserving her uncanny resemblance to the Homeric Hymn's Aphrodite – and this dense literary texture may suffice to justify the disguise. Still, Venus herself draws attention to the puzzlingly unmaternal cast of her behavior by dropping her disguise just as she terminates the interview (402–5):

> Dixit et avertens rosea cervice refulsit,
> ambrosiaeque comae divinum vertice odorem
> spiravere; pedes vestis defluxit ad imos,
> et vera incessu patuit dea.

She finished speaking, and, turning away, shot a gleam from her rosy neck, while her ambrosial tresses breathed out a heavenly fragrance; her dress flowed right down to her feet, and she was revealed by her bearing as a goddess indeed.

The belated revelation provokes Aeneas' resentful questions: "why do you mock your son so often with false semblances, cruel, you too? Why is it not granted to join hand with hand?" (407–9). Why, indeed?

One explanation for Venus' behavior is implicit in the description. Whereas the counterfeit huntress is presented as a collection of appropriate attributes (bow and arrow, athletically hitched-up skirts, nymph's hairstyle), Venus revealed is all about the body's seductive emanations, sheen and scent. It is as if the goddess could only reveal herself as she turns away, thereby shielding her son from a direct confrontation with her irresistible allure. This shielding is the more essential since, as Kenneth Reckford has pointed out, the revelation might otherwise be indecorously complete. The phrase "her dress flowed right down to her feet" implies that Venus has unhitched her dress so as to let it sweep the ground, matron-style. But the phrase could also be understood to mean that she has let her dress drop altogether.[11] Though the first interpretation seems the more likely, this does not mean we ought to discard the other as irrelevant. To the contrary, the oscillation between the two reproduces, in the reader's experience, the fundamental dynamic of the encounter. Behind the matronly image of Venus Genetrix shimmers the

---

[11] Reckford (1996) 1–3.

naked Aphrodite – and this is just Aeneas' problem.[12] As Reckford has demonstrated, the Homeric Hymn to Aphrodite, with its story of the goddess tricking a mistrustful and then reproachful mortal, is a crucial model for the Virgilian encounter, and not just one model among others, but the very origin of the later scene: Aphrodite dresses up as a mortal maiden in order to seduce none other than Anchises, Aeneas' father. Virgil has thus cast Aeneas in his own father's role opposite his ever-youthful mother – in the prelude to his own conception![13]

It is typical of the *Aeneid* that the erotic currents released in this encounter never quite come to rest within individual characters. In the Hymn, the goddess wants to have sex with the mortal, and she compasses this end by veiling both her divinity and her desire: disguising herself as a modest maiden, so that the wary Anchises can discard his anxiety and give way to his own desire. By contrast, the disguise donned by Virgil's Venus does not remove an impediment to desire. To the contrary, by way of the allusion to the Hymn, the disguise introduces a desire that will never be fulfilled. Thus it is not the case that Virgil is discreetly (allusively) depicting a relation of repressed incestuous desire (as if the mother "really" in her heart of hearts harbored a sexual desire for her son, or vice versa). The force of the intertext is rather to bring this desire into the textual economy, where it will be repeatedly but only partially realized, never achieving the literal fruition that would exhaust its productive value.

The most notorious example of quasi-incestuous desire in the epic is the Latin queen Amata's obsession with her prospective son(-in-law) Turnus in the second half of the epic.[14] But the most sustained exploration of this theme is the love affair that the interview between Venus and Aeneas immediately fosters. Indeed, everything takes place as if Venus had resolved to satisfy her incestuous desire by proxy. Not only does she spend much of the interview preparing her son to meet Dido, but she subsequently guarantees the erotic outcome by dispatching Cupid to infect the Carthaginian queen with a fiery passion. Her aim, she confides to Cupid, is that Dido "be held along with me by great love for Aeneas" (*magno Aeneae mecum teneatur amore*, *Aen.* 1.675), a curious expression, in which Reckford identifies "an odd triangle, of sexual passion and

---

[12] Reckford (1996) 3–4, 22.    [13] Reckford (1996) 16–22.    [14] Lyne (1987) 15–17.

(passionate) maternal love." In the event, Dido's passion will be likewise contaminated and will fully merit the reciprocal parenthetical qualification of (maternal).[15]

The composite figure of Cupid and Ascanius that Venus proceeds to deploy against Dido helps compound the cross-generational character of her desire. Instead of having Cupid (Aeneas' half-"brother," as she reminds him, *Aen.* 1.667) use his customary bow and arrows, Venus instructs him to penetrate the palace in the guise of Aeneas' son (Cupid's nephew, if we want to press the logic of the relationship) and to instill his poison directly into the queen. The result is that when Dido takes Cupid-Ascanius into her lap, she effectively embraces two generations in one. The most remarkable sounding of the incestuous note comes in Anna's subsequent reproach to her vacillating sister, already infatuated with Aeneas but still holding out against her desire: "will you know neither sweet children nor the gifts of Venus?" (*nec dulcis natos Veneris nec praemia noris?*, 4.33). Anna is chiding Dido for shunning the marital benefits of offspring and sexual pleasure. But the postponement of the second *nec* to follow *Veneris* means that Anna can also be misheard to say "Will you not know the sweet sons of Venus?" These "sons" (to continue in the path of error) would be Cupid (whom Dido has already unwittingly embraced) and Aeneas (with whom she will be intimately acquainted before the book is out).[16] But what counts most for me here is the way the double-jointed expression, a parapraxis of which Anna is the vehicle but not the author, momentarily merges children with lovers.

If Dido's desire comes from Venus, her fury derives from Juno – hardly a maternal figure. And yet when Dido turns against Aeneas, she is no less the mother. The maternal identification is obliquely vented in the pair of similes that accompanies her nightmare on the eve of Aeneas' departure. A "savage Aeneas" (*ferus Aeneas*, 4.466) "drives" her in solitary "frenzy" (*agit ... furentem*, 465) across the Libyan desert, like a stage Pentheus or Orestes (469–73):

---

[15] Reckford (1996) 25. Cf. Suzuki (1989) 105–6, 117 (re Dido's "almost maternal sympathy," 106).

[16] This (mis)reading is noted with disapproval by Servius ad loc.: *alii male iungunt 'natos Veneris' Cupidinem et Aeneam* (a reference I owe to Richard Thomas).

> Eumenidum veluti demens videt agmina Pentheus
> et solem geminum et duplices se ostendere Thebas,
> aut Agamemnonius scaenis agitatus Orestes,
> armatam facibus matrem et serpentibus atris
> cum fugit ultricesque sedent in limine Dirae.

just as Pentheus in his madness sees ranks of Furies, and the sun twinned, and Thebes showing doubled; or like Agamemnon's son Orestes, harried across the stage, when he flies his mother armed with torches and black snakes, and there on the threshold are encamped the avenging Dirae.

Bracketed by *Eumenidum* and *Dirae*, the Furies in Greek and Latin dress, the passage speaks emphatically to the distraught condition of Dido *furens*. Still, this emphasis is not enough to justify the intrusion of Furies into the tragedy of Pentheus, and certainly not into the memorable scene of Euripides' *Bacchae* that Virgil is rendering here, one featuring Pentheus spellbound by Dionysus, with no Furies in sight. One might describe this as an anticipation error, explained by the subsequent Orestes simile (oh yes, *that's* where the Furies belong). But the introduction of Orestes, a son fleeing the vengeful specter of his mother, also brings into focus a different scene from the tragedy of Pentheus, one that happens later, and offstage: the dismemberment of Pentheus by his own mother, the maddened Agave, in company with her fellow Bacchants. Now here is a scene in which literal or figurative Furies would be quite at home.[17] In her study of mourning mothers, Nicole Loraux asks whether it is "really hazardous for a son to have a mother, and for a mother to have a son?"[18] The bleak alternatives that hover behind this double simile – the son killed by the mother, the mother killed by the son – suggest that the Virgilian answer is "yes."

A hasty reader might be forgiven for identifying Dido *furens* with the infuriated mother and her attendant Furies. Yet the logic of the simile principally aligns her, maddened and fugitive, not with the mother but with the sons. It is true that the dream seems to resist such specifications, opening up as it does a space of fluid identifications (it is this fluidity that

---

[17] As they are in a Pompeian wall painting of this scene, often cited in connection with these lines.

[18] Loraux (1998) 54.

makes it so uncannily mimetic of the actual experience of dreaming): Aeneas not only "drives" Dido (*agit*, 4.465) but, as if anticipating the stagy similes to follow, "plays" her role (another sense of *agere*); and the dazed Pentheus to whom Dido is compared is already cross-dressed for the part, the very image (or so the Euripidean Pentheus coyly hopes) of his own mother – the mother who will shortly tear him limb from limb. It is also true that the interchangeability of Dido and Aeneas is part of the pathos of their relation (both are victims as well as victim-izers, fugitives as well as hunters, etc.); Dido's identification with the troubled sons (even the matricide Orestes appears here in "victim" guise) expresses one dimension of her story.[19] Even so, the perversity of this identification ought not to be too quickly dismissed. After all, just a hundred lines earlier, in her final interview with her faithless lover, Dido looked forward to harassing Aeneas as a shade, one equipped, as if in anticipation of the dream, with the Furies' signature torches (384–6).[20] And later, after Aeneas has set sail, she will entertain a slew of fantasies of extreme revenge (scattering his torn limbs over the sea, serving him Ascanius for dinner) before invoking the "avenging Furies" (*Dirae ultrices*, 610), the same that sit on the threshold of this dream (*ultrices ... Dirae*, 473), to bring her curses to fruition. What the reversed similes occlude but also in their strangeness play up is that Dido hating is just as maternal as Dido in love.

Returning to Aeneas' actual mother, we may ask: is Venus contami-nated by Dido's rage, as Dido by Venus' motherliness? Hardly, it would seem; what one discovers in Venus is not rage but something akin to indifference. By comparison with the Homeric Thetis and Athena, Venus seems strikingly unconcerned about the personal destiny of her epic's hero. She intervenes, true, but not on his account. Her commitment is to the long term and the big picture: the Roman future, and her family's role in shaping it. Accordingly, instead of struggling to prolong Aeneas' life, she proves positively eager to get him armed and into the war which will be the prelude (as Jupiter lets slip at 1.263–6) to his death. When she does reveal herself to him and even (for once!) "seeks her son's embrace" (*amplexus nati Cytherea petivit*, 8.615) it is to fire him with admiration of

---

[19] For Dido as Pentheus (destroyed by the arrival of Aeneas-Dionysus), see further Weber (2002) 333–4.

[20] Cf. Hardie (1993) 41.

his new, divinely wrought armor, and especially the shield, emblazoned with the Augustan future he cannot decipher.[21] The scene is disturbingly reminiscent of Cupid's earlier attack on Dido, likewise carried out via a combination of caresses and splendid gifts, and likewise setting the stage for the recipient's early death. We might consider taking Venus at her word, then, when, in her wounded speech at the divine council of *Aeneid* 10, she sarcastically assents to Aeneas' continuing misfortunes – "as for Aeneas, by all means, let him be tossed about on unknown waves!" (10.48) – on condition that Ascanius be preserved to continue the family line.

As Eleanor Winsor Leach has argued, Virgil's Venus is in many respects an exemplary *matrona*, driven less by motherly affection than by dynastic ambitions, like her real-life contemporaries in the Roman elite.[22] If she is no Thetis, it is because she is a good Roman. Yet there is at least one moment in the epic where Venus' pragmatic indifference seems to screen a darker possibility. As we have seen, in the reproach he aims at her departing back in *Aeneid* 1, Aeneas goes so far as to accuse his mother of cruelty (407–8): "why do you mock your son so often with counterfeit images, cruel, you too?" The phrase "cruel, you too," *crudelis tu quoque*, is imported unaltered from Virgil's eighth eclogue, where it likewise characterizes a mother, possibly Aeneas' own mother, though the reference is notoriously ambiguous. The phrase appears twice in four lines, in a passage that weaves a confusing web of mothers and sons (*Ecl.* 8.47–50):

> saevus Amor docuit natorum sanguine matrem
> commaculare manus; crudelis tu quoque, mater.
> crudelis mater magis, an puer improbus ille?
> improbus ille puer; crudelis tu quoque, mater.

Savage Love taught a mother to stain her hands with her sons' blood; you were cruel too, mother. Who was more cruel, the mother or that wicked boy? That wicked boy; but you were cruel too, mother.

The first mother, the one with the bloodstained hands, is surely Medea, and the twice-addressed "cruel mother" should be Medea too; it is her guilt that matters here. Yet the reiterated coupling of *puer* with *mater*,

[21] Putnam (1995) 43.    [22] Leach (1997).

where the child is unambiguously Amor ( = Cupid), cannot but bring mother Venus to mind.[23] So the question is not whether readers will think of Venus here, but whether (or how quickly) they will banish the thought as irrelevant. It is this composite that glimmers out of Aeneas' reproach, intimating (though Aeneas doesn't know it), howsoever irrationally, that Venus is no less bloodstained a mother than the cruel Medea. Nothing in the action of the poem warrants our accusing Venus of harboring infanticidal impulses, of course, and I am not arguing that Venus, somewhere deep down in her fictional psyche, is "really" hostile to her son. The wisps of hostility trailed by Venus are rather the effects of a mother complex that erupts here and there without taking up residence in any one character.

One of the most intriguing such eruptions is found in the Sicilian interlude of *Aeneid* 5. Though following directly upon the suicide of Dido (it opens with Aeneas at sea looking back at the flames of Dido's pyre), this book is preoccupied with the celebration of funeral games for Anchises, who died in Sicily before Aeneas was blown off course to Dido's shores (the death caps Aeneas' narration of his adventures at 3.708–13). The disjunctive sequence – Dido dies, and Anchises' death is commemorated – produces an effect of corrective censorship, as if the father's honors were aggressively written over the queen's, usurping the space another epic, Punic not Roman, might have devoted to her funeral.[24] In keeping with this chastening, anti-Didonian thrust, the book represents the work of mourning as rigidly segregated, with the men starring in a sequence of competitive displays while the mothers (*matribus*, 5.622; *matres*, 654) weep apart (*procul*, 613).[25] The hypercorrection backfires, however, when the mourning mothers are inspired by Juno's emissary Iris to set fire to the Trojan fleet. Brandishing torches, these "fury-driven" mothers (*actaeque furore*, 659) look strangely like a

---

[23] Discussion in Coleman (1977) 239–40; Servius ad loc. bears witness to the antiquity of the (mis)interpretation.

[24] Virgil's model is the juxtaposition of Hector's death in *Iliad* 22 (largely Trojan-focalized, as *Aeneid* 4 is Dido-focalized) with Patroclus' funeral games in *Iliad* 23. But whereas this disproportion (culminating in the speedy burial of Hector with which the epic concludes) mirrors Achilles' extremes of love and hate, no such character-bound rationale is available in the Virgilian transformation.

[25] On the gender dynamics of *Aen.* 5, see Nugent (1992).

corporate version of the "mother armed with torches" (4.472) before whom Orestes flees in the second simile attending Dido's dream. In this normalization, Dido is now definitively on the side of the Furies, not the son. It is as if these mothers had lit their torches at Dido's funeral pyre, honoring her memory by acting on her fiery fantasies of revenge.[26] Not that the mothers are thinking of Dido; they are evidently preoccupied on the one hand by grief for Anchises, on the other by travel-weariness (*amissum Anchisen flebant*, 5.614; *heu tot vada fessis*, etc., 615ff.). It is not that they identify with Dido, consciously or unconsciously; this is an identification that the text makes for them.

The scene is haunted by the experience not just of Orestes but also and especially of Pentheus. When news of the fire reaches the Trojan menfolk, Ascanius gallops off to bring the mothers to their senses. "What strange new madness is this of yours?" he cries. "It's not a foe, not the enemy camp of the Argives that you are burning, but your own hopes!" (5.670–2). The appeal is punctuated by an emphatic decla-ration and gesture: "'Look, here I am, your Ascanius!' – and he threw his empty helmet down before his feet" (*"en, ego vester | Ascanius!"* – *galeam ante pedes proiecit inanem*, 672–3). The gesture is rendered the more emphatic by the inconsistency of the representation; earlier in this book, the Trojan boys, Ascanius among them, were described as wearing gar-lands, not helmets (556). The helmet is introduced, it seems, just so that it can be removed, yielding a revelation with a particular tragic antecedent: Ascanius is acting the part of the Euripidean Pentheus, who tore the disguising *mitra* from his hair so that his own mother might recognize and spare him (Eur. *Bacch.* 1115–17). The connection is reinforced by the uncanny precision with which Ascanius distills Pentheus' desperate self-identification, "Look, it is I, mother, your child, Pentheus":

ἐγώ **τοι**, μῆτερ, εἰμί, παῖς **σέθεν**

**Πενθεύς**                                    (*Bacch.* 1118–19)

en, ego vester

Ascanius                                      (*Aen.* 5.672–3)

---

[26] So Aeneas' backward glance (*respiciens*, 5.3) at Dido's pyre is answered by the Trojans' (*respiciunt*, 666) at their own ships aflame, with female *furor* to blame in either case (5.6, 670).

Pentheus' pleading does him no good; his mother Agave proceeds to "tear off his shoulder" (ἀπεσπάραξεν ὦμον, *Bacch.* 1127), and the grisly fun begins. Ascanius, by contrast, emerges from his encounter with the Trojan mothers unscathed. Of course, any other outcome would be entirely surreal. The Trojan mothers are not Bacchants primed to tear men apart; they are merely weary travelers who have succumbed, with some prodding from Juno, to their desire to be done with journeying. What makes the Bacchic subtext so intriguing is just this, that it is at once so insistent and so irrelevant.[27] It surfaces where and as it can, in the opportunistic manner of the restless repressed. So the Trojan mothers, chastened by Ascanius' rebuke, "are changed and recognize their own people" (*suosque* / *mutatae agnoscunt*, 5.678–9) – like Agave, painfully restored to her senses by Cadmus at the end of Euripides' *Bacchae*. But their shame also prompts them to "sneak off this way and that to woods and caves" (*silvasque et sicubi concava furtim* / *saxa petunt*, 677–8) – like the Bacchants as Pentheus imagines them early in the tragedy, not shamed but shameless, "slinking off separately into the wild" to have sex with men (*Bacch.* 222–3). A few lines later, faced with the fire that is consuming his fleet, Aeneas prefaces his prayer to Jupiter (duly answered by a rainstorm) with an unusually extravagant gesture of mourning, "tearing" his clothing "off his shoulders," *umeris abscindere vestem* (685) – at once conjuring up and neutralizing Agave's opening attack on Pentheus' shoulder in the Euripidean *sparagmos*. A similar effect is produced by the weirdly redundant characterization of Ascanius' helmet as "void" (*inanem*, 673): "hollow, empty, without a head," as Servius ad loc. patiently explains. No doubt Ascanius kept his head when he threw down his helmet. It is the unnecessary adjective that makes us contemplate the impossible alternative, one realized at the end of the *Bacchae* when the triumphant Agave enters brandishing Pentheus' head impaled on a thyrsus.[28]

Virgil never quite gives us this scene. Yet before the epic is over, the repressed Euripidean intertext will have achieved something perilously

---

[27] The irrelevance is so absolute as to neutralize the insistence; I know of no commentary that notices the traces of Euripides' *Bacchae* here (or in connection with Euryalus and his mother; see futher below).

[28] The thyrsus is mentioned by the messenger (*Bacch.* 1141) though it does not appear in the surviving fragments of the final scene.

close to full expression. The most flamboyant Agave-figure of the *Aeneid* is the Latin queen Amata, an impassioned partisan of Turnus, as we have seen, and the implacable enemy of Aeneas. In *Aeneid* 7, having failed to turn her husband against the Trojan intruder, Amata spirits her daughter away to the mountains, where she is soon joined by other "fury-fired mothers" (*furiisque accensas pectore matres*, 392); the Sicilian scene is now replayed on Italian soil, this time with the mothers as complete Bacchants (389–96): equipped with "ivy stakes" (*pampineas ... hastas*, 396), swathed in animal hides, and chanting the ritual Bacchic cry.[29] No son happens along to meet (or evade) death at the hands of these Bacchants. But the bloody climax is not erased, only displaced and recontextualized to a later book, where a son's head finally makes its appearance, impaled on one of a pair of "stakes" (*hastis*, 9.465) and brandished before a mother's eyes. This is the head of Euryalus, displayed alongside that of Nisus, the two having been caught and killed the previous night while on a mission to summon Aeneas back to Latium. The mother who sees the ghastly spectacle from the walls of the Trojan encampment bursts into lamentation so vehement that she has to be carried away inside, where her grief will not debilitate the surviving warriors.

Granted, it is not a maddened Bacchant but the enemy Rutulians who decapitated these warriors and now vauntingly parade their heads. Even so, the ghosts of Agave and Pentheus hover near this melodramatic confrontation of the mother with the head of her son. It is because she is (not) guilty of Agave's crime that the mother of Euryalus imagines her son as having suffered not just decapitation but *sparagmos*: "What land now holds your limbs, your torn-off parts, your mutilated corpse?" (*quae nunc artus avulsaque membra / et funus lacerum tellus habet?*, 490–1). If not rhetorical, the question would imply that she is contemplating the labor of gathering up the scattered pieces. Earlier, when he tried to rescue the captured Euryalus by launching spears from hiding, Nisus only provoked the enemy to turn on their captive, at which point he sprang into view with a desperately guilty plea: "it's me, me; I'm here, the one who did it; turn your blades against me, Rutulians, all the offence is mine!" (427–8). Is it for nothing that this plea, both its content and its form, is so ostentatiously echoed in the mother's subsequent outburst?

---

[29] Hershkowitz (1998) 50 n. 211: "The *Bacchae* informs the entire episode, with Amata cast in the role of a non-violent Agaue."

"Transfix me," she cries, "hurl all your weapons at me, Rutulians, put me first to the sword!" (493–4).[30] Though the contrastive stress is missing (she means not "kill me instead" but "kill me as well"), she too sounds like a guilty party crying out for punishment.

I would like to conclude this section with one more ambivalently textured Virgilian mother, drawn not from the *Aeneid* but from the *Georgics*. This is the sea-nymph Cyrene, the mother of the prototypical bee-keeper Aristaeus, who turns to her for help after losing his swarm in *Georgics* 4. Cyrene directs him to extract the information he needs from the shape-shifting seer Proteus; and Proteus in turn traces his plight to the anger of Orpheus, whose bride Eurydice died from a snake bite incurred when she was running headlong from Aristaeus (a would-be rapist, it now emerges). Proteus proceeds to tell the story we all know: Orpheus' descent into the underworld, his backward glance and second bereavement, his endless mourning and sexual abstinence, and his consequent death at the hands of Bacchants Virgil identifies as "mothers" (*matres*, 520). The story gets a pragmatic supplement from Cyrene, who tells Aristaeus how to carry out the propitiatory rite that will restore his swarm.

Cyrene is evidently a helpful divine mother, in the tradition of her kinswoman, the sea-nymph Thetis. Yet the emotion she engenders in her son is not filial affection but something more highly charged, a volatile blend of injured love and resentment. The appeal of Aristaeus opens with a stock accusation veiled as a complaint – "Why did you bear me, a scion of the glorious stock of the gods (if my father really is Apollo, as you claim!), to be hated by fate? What has become of your love for me?" (4.322–5) – and culminates in an astonishing explosion of barely concealed aggression (329–32):

> quin age et ipsa manu felicis erue silvas,
> fer stabulis inimicum ignem atque interfice messis,
> ure sata et validam in vitis molire bipennem,
> tanta meae si te ceperunt taedia laudis.

Go on then, why don't you, with your own hand lay my fertile woodlands low, bring fire to wreck the stables, destroy the harvest, burn the crops, and take a mighty ax to the vines, if such revulsion against my glory has taken possession of you.

---

[30] On the strangeness of the echo, see Hardie (1994) 165.

The fantasy of maternal assault reads as the flipside (or Kleinian projection) of the son's own furious fantasy, one that targets, as usual, the fertility of the mother. (Proteus' subsequent reference to Aristaeus' attempted rape of Eurydice will fill out the violent picture with a more conventional content.) Aristaeus' rage is kindled by his inability to monopolize Cyrene's love. And it is true that, as Virgil tells the story, Cyrene is not simply preoccupied with her son. While he is delivering his mournful complaint, she is submerged with her sister nymphs and busy about her sea-green weaving, entertained the while by one of their number, who is singing of "the empty pains of Vulcan, Mars's tricks and sweet thefts" – today's installment in an ongoing enumeration of "the gods' teeming loves, from chaos on" (345–7), a deliciously amoral celebration of adultery unthwarted, theft unpunished, and desire continually reborn. It is because the nymphs are under the spell of this song (*carmine quo captae*, 348) that Cyrene fails at first to respond to her son's complaint. (In the oft-cited parallel of *Iliad* 18, by contrast, Thetis hears Achilles' terrible grief from the depths of the sea and immediately comes to him unbidden.) It is only when Aristaeus renews his complaint (*iterum*, 349) that the spell is broken and Arethusa goes to investigate; and she returns to inform Cyrene that her tearful son is "calling you 'cruel'" (*te crudelem nomine dicit*, 356).

In good Virgilian fashion, the maternal complex vented in Aristaeus' complaint ripples through the rest of the episode without fully surfacing. Aristaeus' resentful hyperbole may enroll Cyrene in the company of "cruel mothers," but the really cruel mothers of *Georgics* 4 are the ones described by Proteus: the ones who tear Orpheus to pieces and scatter his limbs like seeds across the fields (*discerptum latos iuvenem sparsere per agros*, 522). It is these "spurned mothers" (*spretae ... matres*, 520), angered by Orpheus' rejection of their sexual advances, who act out the destructive fantasy Aristaeus entrusts to the mother he feels is spurning him. Moreover, whereas Aristaeus feels slighted by his mother, the very structure of the episode seems designed, like the encounter of mother and son in *Aeneid* 1, to evoke and defuse the contrary danger of too much intimacy. Cyrene thus draws her son into her watery kingdom via the "vast embrace" of her welcoming wave (*accepitque sinu vasto*, 362, where *sinus* overlays the nurse's lap and mother's womb) only to send him off in pursuit of Proteus.

Why Proteus? As many readers have noticed, while this narrative detour is brilliantly productive for the poem, from the perspective of the plot it is undermotivated. It would have been easy enough for Virgil to anchor the excursus more securely in its context (most obviously, by reducing Cyrene's role). As it is, the redundancy (two helpers, two sets of instructions) seems positively to solicit interpretation. For M. Owen Lee, who interprets the episode via the archetypal (Jungian) myth of individuation, there is no redundancy, since Aristaeus needs to discover both "his inner feminine, a complex of mother-memories" and "his inner masculine," the "'Wise Old Man' archetype" embodied in Proteus, the Old Man of the Sea. For Maurizio Bettini, contrariwise, the solution lies in recognizing that Cyrene and Proteus fulfill different narrative functions as, respectively, "donor of magical agent" and "test."[31] In their radically different ways, these are both good answers. But what interests me here is the episode's residual resistance to all such solutions. Cyrene and Proteus *do* overlap, though they needn't have.

The two have distinct and clearly flagged Homeric antecedents; indeed, both are lifted practically straight from Homer. Aristaeus' dealings with his sea-nymph mother are a composite of Achilles' with his sea-nymph mother in *Iliad* 1 and 18, while his wrestling-match with Proteus reenacts Menelaus' contest with the identical slippery divinity in *Odyssey* 4. Thus within the intertextual repertoire constituted by the Aristaeus episode, Thetis bumps up against Proteus. And this juxtaposition may bring to mind another famous contest between a mortal and an elusive marine deity, the one featuring not Proteus but Thetis: the sexual contest in which Peleus vanquished his shape-shifting bride, an encounter of which Achilles was the fruit. As in *Aeneid* 1, albeit at a further remove, the hero's encounter with his mother is intertextually shadowed by the possibility of incest, and of the most primordial kind: the assumption of the father's role at the scene of his own conception. Aristaeus is not wrestling knowledge out of his mother, of course (any more than the Aeneas of *Aeneid* 1 is preparing to have sex with his). Yet the doubling of Cyrene by Proteus conjures up the specter of incest as it wards it off.

As I noted at the outset, the project of this chapter swims against, or at least tacks across, the prevailingly patriarchal current of Roman literature and culture. This is a current that has fostered, I want to

---

[31] Lee (1996) 103; Bettini (1991) 239.

underscore, a very rich tràdition of father-centered readings. In David Quint's powerful account of the *Aeneid*, for example, mastering the traumatic past, the essential task for Aeneas and Augustus alike, centrally involves coming to terms with the (psychological, ideological) problem posed by the father. So, for Quint, "[t]he whole first half of the *Aeneid* may be read as an attempt to deal with the father and the past that he represents."[32] The thrust of Quint's reading is political but the story has obvious metaliterary implications: the burden of the Trojan past, one Aeneas literally shoulders as he exits Troy with his father perched on his neck, answers to the overwhelming weight of the Homeric tradition shouldered by the poet of the *Aeneid* in his quest to found Homeric epic anew in Italy. This correspondence has been fruitfully explored via the thematics of filial and poetic "succession" by Philip Hardie, who concludes that Latin epic offers relatively hospitable ground for a Bloomian exploration of "the anxiety of influence."[33] And no ground more hospitable, it would seem, than the funeral games of Anchises in *Aeneid* 5, a depiction of agonistic sport ostentatiously designed to rival the funeral games of *Iliad* 23; as Joseph Farrell has remarked, "*Aeneid* 5 appears to be an ideal instantiation of everything Harold Bloom means when he speaks of literary influence as a process closely akin to Freud's notion of what takes place in the mind of a son trying to imagine himself as a father."[34] For Llewelyn Morgan, the Aristaeus section of *Georgics* 4 supplies an early chapter in this metapoetic story: the quest of Aristaeus is an initiatory exercise in which poet and hero participate simultaneously. A key detail in Morgan's reading is the libation Cyrene pours to Ocean, "father of all things" (*patrem rerum*, *Geo.* 4.382) and a conventional figure for Homer, "the origin of all literature" (as Morgan puts it).[35] Aristaeus' descent into the paternal waters thus figures Virgil's immersion in his great "source" while also prefiguring the upcoming *agon* in which Aristaeus masters Proteus, as Virgil Homer.[36]

The paternal current naturally sets toward an allegory of literary creation featuring the poet as a father's son, whether gratefully inheriting, or aggressively claiming, or anxiously negotiating, the legacy of his

[32] Quint (1993) 50–96 (citation from 57).

[33] Hardie (1993) 98–119 (116–19 on Bloom).    [34] Farrell (1999) 103.

[35] Morgan (1999) 32.    [36] Morgan (1999) 48–9.

poetic progenitor. But this is not the only story that can be told about poetic origins. Here I take my cue from Farrell, who offers his Bloomian evaluation of *Aeneid* 5 only in order to qualify it: "Is the 'greater part' of the book in fact a literary and metaliterary agon between pairs of fathers and sons, Anchises and Aeneas, Homer and Vergil? Or does this formulation leave something out?"[37] An answer is forthcoming a few pages later. *Aeneid* 5 may be dedicated to Aeneas' mortal father, but Virgil never quite lets us forget that the real power rests with Aeneas' immortal mother: "the subtext of Book 5 tends to inscribe paternity within a more dominant theme of motherhood."[38] In his early essay on Freud, Kenneth Burke remarked a similar "overemphasis upon the patriarchal pattern" in Freudian theory and insisted, like Farrell, that we need to pay more attention to mothers. By way of example, Burke pointed to the profusion of rebirth rituals in what he calls "the literature of transitional eras" and suggested that such rituals would tend "to be completed by symbolizations of matricide."[39] It is not just the father, then, but the mother who sets a problem for both the poet and the hero to solve.

Does Virgil's poetry supply the makings of a maternal supplement to the paternal allegory, Homer the mother, as it were?[40] If so, what might such a supplement look like? To imagine the literary origin as a mother would be to imagine a model of literary influence keyed not to agonistic competition (still less to some utopian vision of maternal plenitude) but to the complementary dangers of absorption and *sparagmos*. One scatters the mother-text so as not to be scattered or swallowed up by her.[41] What I like about this model is that it answers to

---

[37] Farrell (1999) 103.     [38] Farrell (1999) 108.

[39] Burke ([1939] 1973) 273, 274, in the course of a typically engaging exploration of Freud's value for literary criticism.

[40] So Dante will figure Virgil as his mother near the end of *Purgatorio* (a reference I owe to Simone Marchesi). Is it just a happy accident that the nymph who delights Cyrene and her fellow-weavers with a song about (pro)creation bears (according to one tradition; see Thomas (1988) 210) the name of Homer's mother?

[41] This is a Kleinian fable, albeit one that Klein would not embrace. For Klein, creativity springs from "the desire to make reparation" to the mother who has been destroyed in fantasy: the artwork restores the mother by putting her back together. By contrast, "envy of creativeness" (especially the mother's) is "a fundamental element in the disturbance of the creative process." See Klein ([1929] 1975) 218, ([1957] 1975) 202.

Virgil's practice of producing his own text out of the bits and pieces of his "mother"-texts.[42] Some may object to this as an illicit psychologiza-tion of Virgil's intensely self-conscious art. But I mean it rather as another self-reflexive scenario, one no more and no less psychically charged than the more familiar oedipal story. I do not have a myth handy to attach to this model; in Greek literature sons do not rip up their mothers. (The matricidal Orestes comes the closest, and it is not very close.)[43] But it may be that the recurrent story of the son (call him Orpheus, call him Pentheus) succumbing to the violent hands of the mother covers over, serves to motivate, and itself figures, the son's assault on the mother. Recently Farrell has written about the prolifer-ation of elaborate intertextual programs, more or less fragmentary or comprehensive, that have been detected in the *Aeneid*, involving not just Homer, but Apollonius of Rhodes; and Aeschylus' *Oresteia*; add Sophocles' *Ajax*, Euripides' *Bacchae* and *Hippolytus*; and we can be confident that the list is not complete.[44] At issue is not (just) the insane desire of scholars to trace Virgil's innumerable sources; nothing really comparable has been practiced on the poetry of Horace or Ovid, for instance. It is as if Virgil had plunged into the very matrix of textuality, and had taken his readers with him.

## The mother's tongue: Ovid's Philomela and the birth of *libertas*

The Ovidian story to which I turn next carries the argument from the lurid fantasies of Kleinian infancy to more familiar, albeit in the end no less lurid, Freudian territory. Such a claim may seem perverse, given that

---

[42] Cf. Most (1992) (on the correlation of textual and bodily "members"). For a sparagmatic account of Virgilian intratextuality, see Oliensis (2004).

[43] In her essay on the *Oresteia*, Klein analyzes Orestes (he illustrates "the transition between the paranoid-schizoid and the depressive position," Klein ([1963] 1975) 286) but refrains from turning him into a paradigm. For an attempt to replace Oedipus with Orestes, taking matricide as the foundational act of patriarchal culture, see Irigaray (1991) 34–46. Residual traces of matricide in the *Aeneid*: Oliensis (2001) 60. As Seth Schein points out to me, the most apt myth is supplied by the Babylonian *Enuma Elish*, which gives us Marduk creating the world out of the dismembered body of Tiamat.

[44] Farrell (2005).

my chosen episode, the story of Philomela, Procne, and Tereus that fills the second half of *Metamorphoses* 6, deals directly with the material that breaks sporadically into the *Aeneid*: a mother who dismembers her son. In fact, Procne is *the* infanticidal mother of the *Metamorphoses*, filling in for Medea (whose maternal crime receives the briefest of mentions in the subsequent book), and reprising and expanding the role of Agave from the end of *Metamorphoses* 3.[45] But Procne is not the mother with whom I am principally concerned; it is not Procne but her sister, the childless Philomela, who stars in the maternal tale I have now to unfold. And my subject is no longer what the son fears from the mother but what the mother sees in him – or rather (taking a hard line on the masculinist bias of Freudian theory) what he fears she sees. But for the time being I want to leave that complicating qualification to one side.

A brief review of the Ovidian episode is in order. The story begins with the girls' father, Pandion of Athens, consolidating his alliance with the Thracian king Tereus by marrying him to Procne. The newlyweds depart for Thrace, are blessed with a baby boy, and live uneventfully for five years, until Procne is possessed by longing for her sister Philomela. Dispatched to fetch her, Tereus is overwhelmed by desire for the sister and, on their return to Thrace, takes her into the depths of the forest and rapes her; when she threatens to broadcast his crime to the world, he cuts out her tongue, thereafter returning to Procne with a feigned report of Philomela's death en route. After a year imprisoned in the forest, Philomela sends her sister a tapestry communicating her story; Procne then rescues her sister and punishes Tereus by feeding their son Itys to him for dinner, after which the three protagonists are transformed into birds.

The story is saturated with what Charles Segal has termed "the terrible mimetic violence of the revenge plot," with Tereus' rape of Philomela answered, both punished and duplicated, by Procne's murder of Itys.[46] Indeed, the stringent demands of poetic justice are such as to cast Tereus not merely as a rapist but as a virtual father violating his "daughter," as if only this crime could be sufficient to motivate the mother's subsequent "violation" of her son. The incestuous identification notoriously originates with Tereus himself: avidly watching Philomela as she

[45] The other relevant mother is Althaea (featured in *Met.* 8), though her crime is distinctly less grisly.

[46] Segal (1994b) 272.

embraces her father, Tereus "could wish he were the father" (*esse parens vellet*, 6.482), a wish ironically seconded by an unwitting Pandion when he entreats his departing son-in-law to watch over Philomela with "a father's love" (*patrio …. amore*, 499). But the identification also breaks the surface as a sort of irrational pun or parapraxis when "king" (Tereus) drags "Pandion's daughter" (Philomela) into the forest, *cum rex Pandione natam* (520), a phrase that flashes a rapist named "king Pandion" before our eyes. Likewise, when Tereus cuts out Philomela's tongue, it is "repeatedly calling out the name of father" (*nomen patris usque vocantem*, 555) – the father she hopes may come to her rescue, of course, but also and antithetically the unthinkably violent father who stands before her; the latter, latent sense is retroactively guaranteed by the mirror scene of Procne's revenge, where Itys is "crying 'mother, mother!'" (*"mater, mater" clamantem*, 640) as Procne gears up for the slaughter.

Itys' reiterated appeal is directed toward Procne, of course, not toward Philomela, though the mute sister is also present on the scene (ready to cut Itys' throat after Procne inflicts the death blow). The incestuous subtext pegs Philomela as the daughter of a father, not the mother of a son; the latter role is reserved for Procne. And of course the mythological Philomela, a character with whom Ovid's readers would have been well acquainted, especially from the tragic stage, never does have a child.[47] Still, it must be remarked that Philomela's exclusion from motherhood is one of the stranger features of the episode as Ovid has written it. As a literary event, rape conventionally yields offspring; it is this that makes rape narratable, and worth narrating. The point is driven home at the start of *Metamorphoses* 6, in the sequence of divine rapes represented on the tapestry Arachne weaves in her contest with Minerva – rapes uniformly destined to bear fruit (as the narrator intermittently reminds us: Jupiter "filled Antiope full with twins," 111; Neptune "begets the Aloidae," 117, etc.).[48] It is true that the Philomela story is the first in the

---

[47] Or rather, the raped sister (whatever her name) never does have a child; in some versions the names are interchanged (an ominous symptom of the ease with which they can be confounded, e.g., by Tereus).

[48] And in the next episode (Niobe vs. Latona) maternal procreativity is itself the matter of contention; the theme may also reverberate in the transformations of Arachne and the Lycian peasants (whose story follows Niobe's) into spider and frogs respectively, creatures famous for spawning innumerable young (a suggestion I owe to Lesley Dean-Jones).

poem involving mortals only (the episode is identified as a major juncture in the poem for just this reason), and that Tereus' failure to plant a
child in Philomela functions as an index of the difference between gods
and mortals (divine sex being, by contrast, invariably productive).[49] But
the story seems designed to draw particular attention to this failure.
As the narrator informs us, even after cutting out Philomela's tongue,
Tereus returned to inflict his desire on her maimed body, not once but
"often" (*saepe*, 562). The ghastly and gratuitous detail, which the narrator ostentatiously disavows ("so they say (I'd scarcely venture to
believe it)," *(vix ausim credere) fertur*, 561), certainly underscores
Tereus' barbarity. But it also (and I suspect this is its primary function)
furnishes multiple opportunities for impregnation. How can it be that
these repeated encounters yield no fruit?

As if in response to this subterranean current, the narrator prefaces
his next mention of Philomela with an announcement of the passage of
"twice six months" (6.571), an interval that might herald the announcement of the birth of a child. Naturally, it does not; as noted above, the
story of Philomela cannot accommodate a pregnancy. Accordingly,
what this lengthy gestation produces is not a child but a brainchild: the
tongueless Philomela is inspired to denounce her assailant by weaving
her story into a tapestry. The figurative equivalence of tapestry and child
is anticipated by the juxtaposed dooms of Arachne and Niobe, brilliant
weaver and prolific mother, at the start of *Metamorphoses* 6 (Ovid is in
any case very fond of the trope artwork = offspring). But Philomela's
tapestry substitutes for her child in another sense too. In the world of
Ovid's poem, and beyond it, one function of such a child is to provide
incontrovertible evidence of the crime that produced it. When Callisto,
raped by Jupiter nine months previously, strips down to swim with her
fellow nymphs, she exposes to Diana's furious gaze "her crime together
with her naked body" (*nudo patuit cum corpore crimen*, 2.462); the
hapless victim subsequently provokes Juno's resentment as well by giving birth, thereby (Juno complains) "publicizing the wrong and bearing
witness to my Jove's dishonor" (*fieretque iniuria partu / nota Iovisque
mei testatum dedecus esset*, 472–3). Semele is likewise assailed by the
much-injured queen of Olympus for fleshing out Jupiter's adulterous

---

[49] As Poseidon assures Tyro at *Od.* 11.248–50 (with thanks to Olga Levaniouk for the
reference).

inclinations for all to see: "she bears the crime in plain view in her full belly" (*manifestaque crimina pleno | fert utero*, 3.268–9).[50] Like Arachne's tapestry, with its vivid array of what Minerva views as "divine crimes" (*caelestia crimina*, 6.131), Philomela's tapestry bears "intelligence of a crime" (*indicium sceleris*, 578), thereby fulfilling the evidentiary function of the child it has displaced.

This is Philomela's most successful but not her first attempt at testifying against Tereus. Immediately after the rape, having recovered with remarkable rapidity from her initial prostration and terror, Philomela delivers herself of an inexplicably eloquent speech, an impassioned denunciation culminating in a fearless promise of *indicium* to come (6.544–7):

> ipsa pudore
> proiecto tua facta loquar. si copia detur,
> in populos veniam; si silvis clausa tenebor,
> implebo silvas et conscia saxa movebo.

I myself, with modesty cast aside, will say what you have done; should the opportunity be granted, I will come before the nations; if I am shut up fast in the forest, I will fill the forest full and rouse the very rocks, made partners of my knowledge.

Worse than useless, the speech serves only to arouse the anger and fear of Tereus, who proceeds to render Philomela incapable of delivering on her threat by removing her defiant tongue. But Philomela's eloquence is not just impolitic, it is also unconventional in the extreme. It is regularly the woman, not the man, who suffers the stigma of rape; once her modesty has been violated, the woman's part is to repair the damage by covering herself back up, not to exacerbate it by making her injury public.

As in the Arachne episode (long a magnet for political readings), so too here the anomalous indictment of the man by the woman contributes to an occult political resonance. The very untimeliness of the speech contributes to its emblematic quality, making it something less used than

---

[50] Whose "crime"? Juno's fudging of the issue is especially clear in the case of Callisto; she comes close to acknowledging that the "wrong" was done to Callisto by Jupiter, but immediately suppresses this possibility by turning around and ascribing the *dedecus*, most implausibly, to the rapist ("dishonor" is the lot of the raped woman, cf. *Fast.* 2.826, discussed below).

mentioned, an exemplary and excerptable specimen of dauntless out-spokenness. Its value is retroactively guaranteed, moreover, by the extreme violence of the censorship it provokes. Not for nothing is Tereus described at precisely this juncture as a "savage tyrant" (*feri* ... *tyranni*, 6.549). One thinks especially of Cicero, already a legendary figure just a few decades after he paid with his life, and with his eloquent head and hands, for the unbridled freedom of his *Phil(omel)ippics*. Cicero was likewise associated with a "tongue" in the eulogies his death inspired: "I must mourn Cicero and the silence of the Latin tongue" (*deflendus Cicero est Latiaeque silentia linguae*), proclaimed Sextilius Ena; "sorrow-stricken, the eloquence of the Latin tongue fell sadly silent" (*ictaque luctu | conticuit Latiae tristis facundia linguae*), lamented Cornelius Severus.[51] An otherwise unexceptional metonymy for "speech" or "language," these "tongues" are uneasily surcharged with meaning by the specter of the orator's severed head. It is this latent corporeality that comes to the fore in Philomela's tongue, a grotesque embodiment of Ciceronian eloquence literally cut off.[52] The political allegory may also be read (need not be read, but remains available) in Philomela's subsequent turn from candid public speaking to the covert communication of her tapestry, with its "red marks" woven into "white threads" (*purpureasque notas filis intexuit albis*, 577; *notae* can suggest a private code): individual ingenuity will always find a way to circumvent tyrannical censorship, no matter how violently imposed.[53]

This turn from speech to writing sets in higher relief the value of the original issue of the rape. It emerges that Tereus did unwittingly beget something on the body of Philomela: not offspring but speech; not *liberi* but *libertas*. The foundational value of this pun comes into sharper focus when we recognize Philomela's kinship with Lucretia, another raped woman, and one most intimately associated with the birth of political liberty at Rome. That the two stories are filed together in Ovid's imagination is evident from *Fasti* 2, where the rape of Lucretia is bracketed by

---

[51] Seneca the Elder, *Suas.* 6.26–7. On the implications of Cicero's mutilation, see Richlin (1999) (with a discussion of the tongue, including Philomela's, at 202–6).

[52] On Philomela's tongue, "at once an organ ... and 'language,'" see the suggestive discussion of Enterline (2000) 88–90 (citation from 89).

[53] Like Cicero, Philomela spreads a contagion of muteness: when Procne "reads" the tapestry, her tongue fails to find words (*verbaque quaerenti satis indignantia linguae | defuerunt*, 6.584–5).

allusions to the tragedy of Philomela.[54] That they were filed together in the Roman imagination is evident from the politic substitution of Accius' *Tereus* for his *Brutus* at the Ludi Apollinares put on by Brutus *in absentia* in the summer of 44 BCE (Rome was too hot for the assassins): if a play featuring the original Liberator (Brutus' choice) was too transparent, *Tereus* would serve as well to elicit a demonstration of popular support for the contemporary champion of liberty (as Cicero reports that it did).[55] In Livy's canonical version of the Lucretia story, the two senses of *libertas*, unconstrained speech and freedom from despotic rule, are tightly interwoven. The rapist's first word, when he appears at Lucretia's bedside, is the imperative *tace*: "'Silence, Lucretia,' says he; 'I am Sextus Tarquin; the sword is in my hand; you'll die, if you make a sound'" (*moriere, si emiseris vocem*, 1.58). This violently imposed silence is undone first by Lucretia herself, who denounces the rapist to her menfolk the next morning, and then by Brutus, who translates her call for vengeance into a political revolution. One of Brutus' first actions after expelling the Tarquins is to oversee the execution of his own sons, exposed as Tarquin-sympathizers; it is only by ceasing to be the father of flesh-and-blood sons (potentially a new line of tyrants; Brutus is himself a Tarquin by blood) that Brutus confirms his standing as the "father" of liberty.[56] By annihilating the son the tyrant may have planted in her, Lucretia's suicide likewise enables the birth of the free Republic. Hence *liberi*, not "children" but "free," broaches Livy's second book (*Liberi iam hinc populi Romani res pace belloque gestas*, 2.1).

Ovid seems to have city foundations very much in mind in *Metamorphoses* 6. The book opens, let us recall, with the contest between Minerva and Arachne, and Minerva's tapestry, which is described first, represents another contest, "an ancient quarrel over naming the land" (*antiquam de terrae nomine litem*, 6.71); Minerva's olive tree was judged superior to Neptune's salty spring, and the nameless territory was accordingly placed under her patronage and her name. This charter myth of the birth of Athens was depicted on the west pediment of the Parthenon, the east pediment being occupied by the birth of Athena herself from the head of Zeus, an event that perhaps reverberates in

[54] Newlands (1995) 162.
[55] Cic. *Phil.* 1.36. Brutus' original plan: Cic. *Att.* 16.5.1, with Ramsey (2003) 151–2.
[56] Feldherr (1997) 142–4.

Minerva's subsequent assault on the head of Arachne ("three times and four she smote the brow of Idmon's daughter," *ter quater Idmoniae frontem percussit Arachnes*, 133).[57] Roman history too featured an originary contest over "who should give his name to the new city" (*qui nomen novae urbi daret*, Livy 1.6), one that Romulus ambiguously won from his perch atop the Palatine.[58] Add to this the association of Philomela with Lucretia, and it begins to look as if *Metamorphoses* 6 were playing at recasting Athenian history, from the legendary foundation down to the violent birth pangs of the democracy, in a Roman mold.[59]

Yet there are tensions around the heroic figure of the *mater patriae*. Denouncing the assailant, as I noted earlier, is not the woman's part. If Livy's exemplary Lucretia can do so, it is because she speaks with an almost impersonal authority, as if from beyond the grave to which she is about to consign herself. The elegiac Lucretia of Ovid's *Fasti* is more "realistic" in that she can hardly speak even before a sympathetic family audience: she hides her face and weeps in shame, and when she finally manages to communicate part of her story (veiling the obscene end in renewed tears and blushes), the first accusation she levels against Tarquin is precisely that he has forced her to proclaim her own dishonor herself (*"hoc quoque Tarquinio debebimus, eloquar," inquit, | "eloquar infelix dedecus ipsa meum?", Fast.* 2.825–6). Moreover, neither Livy's manly nor Ovid's womanly Lucretia, nor their immediate family, contemplates publishing the domestic scandal to the world. It is the revolutionary Brutus who, by broadcasting what Ovid terms "the king's unspeakable deeds" (*regis facta nefanda*, 2.850), both exercises and founds the *libertas* of the infant Republic. By contrast, the violated Philomela of Ovid's *Metamorphoses* herself assumes the role of a Brutus, a Cicero. Far from gathering up the tattered shreds of her injured

---

[57] The promotion of father "Idmon" ( = Knower) suggests that the scene perverts a traditional allegory of the birth of wisdom. Minerva likewise "smites" the earth when she generates her olive-"child": *percussamque sua simulat de cuspide terram | edere cum bacis fetum canentis olivae* (6.80–1). The olive is born complete with fruit, as Minerva completely armed (as she depicts herself here: see 78–80); Minerva seems obsessed with replaying the scene of her own birth.

[58] It may not be by chance that Minerva regularly appears as "Pallas" in *Met.* 6.

[59] An enterprise all the bolder in that the Lucretia story was itself patterned on an Athenian story (Harmodius and Aristogeiton) associating tyrannical desire, resistance, and democratic revolution.

*pudor*, in her determination to expose the tyrant to the world at large, she is prepared to jettison modesty altogether.

Surely Philomela makes an admirable, even heroic display of courage. And yet for a woman to speak *pudore proiecto*, as Philomela promises to do (6.544–5), is to risk speaking shamelessly, irrevocably dirtying her tongue. The danger is illustrated earlier in *Metamorphoses* 6 by the hubristic Niobe, whom Latona accuses of deploying her "father's tongue" (*linguam ... paternam*, 213) – a tongue worthy of Niobe's criminal father Tantalus, she means – in heaping "abuse" (*convicia*, 210) on the goddess and her twins. It is illustrated again in the next episode, in still more lurid colors, by the Lycian peasants, likewise specialists in "abuse" (*convicia*, 362), who even as frogs continue to "exercise their foul tongues in quarrels" (*turpes | litibus exercent linguas*) and, "with modesty routed" (*pulsoque pudore*), preserve even underwater their habit of "badmouthing" (*maledicere*, 374–6). Philomela is neither a madly boastful aristocrat nor a foul-tongued peasant, of course. But what these unsavory episodes underscore is that the value accorded to speech is a function of the social identity of the speaker. If Philomela's tongue, unlike Cicero's head and hands, never came to be a nostalgic emblem of lost *libertas*, it is not only because of the gory revenge she takes in the horrendous sequel. A woman cannot speak out publicly, above all of her own violation, without violating the most fundamental rules of decorum.

The episode thus presents, alongside the Lucretia-style discourse on the origins of *libertas*, a familiar misogynist discourse on the essential impropriety of women's speech. An emblematic text in this discourse is a fragmentary fable by Phaedrus: when Prometheus was fashioning humankind, he made the woman's tongue right after (or from?) the man's genitals (*a fictione veretri linguam mulieris*, 4.15). Hence the innate obscenity of female speech: the woman who plies her tongue usurps the man's part.[60] In *Metamorphoses* 6, this part is especially associated with the father. When Latona complains of the "father's tongue" exhibited by Niobe, she also names the virile organ deployed by

---

[60] Phaedr. 4.15. The sense of the scanty remains is disputed, but the general thrust seems clear enough; on the tongue–penis "similarity," see Adams (1982) 35 (citing this passage).

Philomela, in the absence of a father-protector, against her paternal assailant. Before raping Philomela, Tereus takes a moment to "confess the crime" to come, *fassusque nefas* (524) – to "speak the unspeakable," in Ovid's etymologizing pun. The curious detail (Tereus was wildly impatient of delay before this) seems included as an anticipation of Philomela's transgression: now it is she who will venture to speak the unspeakable.

The default reader of this episode is doubtless meant to condemn Tereus as he gloats in advance over his victim, and to applaud Philomela as she confronts her barbaric foe. But a jury of Tereus' Thracians might respond differently. It is not just that Philomela will have to dirty her mouth by speaking of the rape. A hostile audience might already detect the obscene tones of the phallus in Philomela's promise, "shame cast aside" (*pudore / proiecto*, 6.544–5) and (sexual) "access" granted (*copia*, 545), to "enter" the nations (*in populos veniam*, 546), "impregnate" the woods, and "stir up" the rocks (*implebo silvas et conscia saxa movebo*, 547). This tendentious perspective infiltrates Ovid's startling description of Tereus "liberating" his sword from its sheath (*vagina liberat ensem*, 551) as he prepares, virtuously as it were, to deprive Philomela of the part she has foully usurped.[61] The *kakemphaton* is amplified by the image of the severed tongue, writhing on the ground like "a maimed snake's tail" (*mutilatae cauda colubrae*, 559), as if externalizing the "tail"[62] Tereus had unwittingly left behind.

The tongue is not only an errant emblem of masculine privilege, however. If Philomela's outburst is emblematic of *libertas*, her severed tongue figures its premature demise; superimposed upon the castrated phallic tongue is an aborted child. The identification of penis with child is a psychoanalytic topos, of course; for Freud, the birth of a son assuages the mother's penis envy by making up for what she lacks. But the identification is also perfectly Roman. Niobe's abuse focuses on Latona's meager procreative output as compared to her own maternal

---

[61] This confounding phrase, issuing here as if from the Thracian perspective, recurs at *Fast.* 2.793 in connection with the rapist Tarquin (the liberator Brutus has to make do with the verb *rapit*, 838). On the dizzying temporal conflations produced by this episode (Brutus as liberator/Brutus as assassin), see Newlands (1995) 169–70.

[62] The original meaning of Latin *penis*; *cauda* ( = penis) also in Horace's *Satires*. See Adams (1982) 35–7.

fecundity, and her subsequent punishment certainly cuts her down to size. Yet what makes this act of justice "poetic," what makes the punishment fit the crime, is that it attacks the tally of the part that sinned: taking the children in place of the wagging paternal tongue. Of course, Tereus will suffer likewise for *his* wagging "tongue," forfeiting his progeny, as Niobe hers, to an implacable pair of vengeful siblings.[63]

It is in Tereus' son Itys that the association of phallus, child, and tongue reaches its clotted climax. In Livy's history, the birth of the Republic is a triumph of abstraction, enabled by the movement from inside to outside and the replacement of actual by symbolic motherhood. Ovid's tragedy ends by reversing this movement, netting the figurative within its literal fulfillment: a real child. From Philomela's *libertas*, to her tapestry, to Itys, the text travels back toward embodiment. And the culmination of this movement is the reincorporation of the child within the parent's body, as the banqueting Tereus "piles his own flesh and blood into his own belly" (*inque suam sua viscera congerit alvum*, 6.651). Procne's viciously playful reply to Tereus' subsequent summoning of Itys – "inside you have the one you ask for," *intus habes quem poscis* (655) – is likewise marked by material excess, harboring not only a double sense ("inside" the house/"inside" your body) but the very name of "Itys"/*intus*.[64] This thickening corporealization of language, the reflex of an aborted *libertas*, peaks when Tereus once again asks for Itys. This time it is Philomela's turn to answer (656–9):

> quaerenti iterumque vocanti,
> sicut erat sparsis furiali caede capillis
> prosiluit Ityosque caput Philomela cruentum
> misit in ora patris.

He asking and calling him again, just as [she/it] was, hair streaming with furious slaughter, Philomela leaped forth and hurled the bloody head of Itys into the father's face.

---

[63] Tereus and Philomela thus share an identification with Niobe, just as Tereus and Procne share an identification with Apollo vis-à-vis Philomela-Diana. On Tereus' resemblance to the Apollo of *Met.* 1 (infatuated with the Diana-clone Daphne), see Jacobsen (1984); on the lesbian (and incestuous) undertones released by these proliferating structural correspondences, see Brown (2005) 89–101.

[64] I owe this crypt word to John Shoptaw.

One may wonder whose "hair" is "streaming" here: Philomela's, or the hair on the "bloody head" she is carrying? The same confusion shapes the next line, which momentarily pictures Itys himself leaping into view, *prosiluit Ity-*, until the nominative resolves into the genitive and one head detaches itself from the other. It is as if Philomela were wearing the head of Itys like a mask. But this head not only doubles Philomela's head, it functions as her surrogate tongue. In her answer to Tereus' question, "where is Itys?," Philomela replaces the name with the thing, speaking the primitive language of objects, "emitting" the head as if it were a word. Not that this material communication sates Philomela's desire (never more acute than at this moment, Ovid tells us) for the voice and words with which to "bear witness" not to his crime but to her joy. Ovid knows better than most the pleasure language, mere language, can afford.

## *Mater patriae?*

Philomela's progressively more perverse variations on maternity are released by a rupture of narrative logic. It is because she is not a mother that she becomes so variously a "mother": in her exemplary or obscene advocacy of *libertas*; in her gestation of a tapestry in place of a child; and finally in her substitution of the body of a real child for the communications of tongue and text. Lacking the essential virile complement afforded by a Brutus, Philomela travels Lucretia's path in reverse, overseeing the devolution of public *libertas* into the most incestuously private of kinship relations: the father's reincorporation of his son.

Yet it is worth remarking that Lucretia, though cast in this role by the figurative argument of Livy's history, is never identified as the "mother" of the Republic. Roman ideology includes the ideal of the *pater patriae* (a title with which Cicero and Augustus were both honored) but offers no complementary title on the maternal side.[65] The accounts of Lucretia's heroism tend rather to masculinize her (hers is "a manly soul by a cruel error of fortune allotted a woman's body," according to Valerius Maximus), as if her procreative capacity could only be a hindrance to the new

---

[65] Or not till much later; the Senate's attempt so to honor Livia was quashed by Tiberius; see Tac. *Ann.* 1.14.1.

order she fosters.[66] There is, however, one mother indubitably associated with the origins of Rome, and that is the goddess Cybele, "Great Idaean Mother of the Gods," as she was titled at Rome, whose worship was imported into the city from the Phrygian east, along with her outlandish priests, the castrated *galli*, near the end of the second Punic War.[67] The Magna Mater appears in one of the most ideologically charged passages of the *Aeneid*, Aeneas' encounter with the shade of Anchises, who shows him the souls of Rome's future heroes pacing across the underworld landscape of *Aeneid* 6. When Romulus comes into view, Anchises interrupts his running commentary on the parade to insert an advertisement for the city Romulus will found: "under his auspices, my son, will that glorious Rome make her dominion equal the world, her spirit match Olympus" (*en huius, nate, auspiciis illa incluta Roma / imperium terris, animos aequabit Olympo*, 781–2). And Anchises proceeds to associate the coming world power, "blessed with virile progeny" (*felix prole virum*, 784), with the turret-crowned Cybele (786–7):

> laeta deum partu, centum complexa nepotes,
> omnis caelicolas, omnis supera alta tenentis.

happy in her divine offspring, embracing a hundred descendants, all of them inhabitants of heaven, all dwelling in the heights above.

Here at last, it seems, is a benign vision of public maternity, aptly yoking, as Vassiliki Panoussi puts it, the "positive, non-threatening" mother-goddess with the world-embracing mother Roma.[68] As Panoussi's adjectives imply, moreover, it takes a certain expenditure of energy to produce such a vision: the Great Mother is also wont to appear not positive and nonthreatening but negative and threatening, with her retinue of *castrati* serving as a flamboyant reminder of her fearful might. It is this problematic counter-image that Virgil's simile overwrites, and thoroughly too. Flanked as she is on one side by Romulus, on the other by Julius Caesar and his world-conquering heir, this Magna Mater seems unimpeachably

---

[66] *virilis animus maligno errore fortunae muliebre corpus sortitus*, Val. Max. 6.1.

[67] The association of *Roma* with *ruma* "teat" (that of the wolf who nursed the fabled twins) likewise supplies a national motherhood removed from any human mother. On the antiquity of the etymology, see Rochette (1997); for Shakespeare's variations on this Roman theme, Adelman (forthcoming).

[68] Panoussi (2003) 122.

Augustan, harboring none of the exotic madness with which previous generations had associated her.[69]

Yet even in this triumphalist setting, the motherhood celebrated by father Anchises expresses a residual disquiet. Elsewhere in the epic, the Magna Mater casts a shadow on the reputation of Aeneas and his fellow Trojans, whom hostile invective regularly assimilates to the goddess's emasculated Phrygian attendants,[70] and one may glimpse this same shadow flickering across the bright future of Anchises' depiction. Emasculation may seem the very antithesis of the world dominion foretold by Anchises. But the self-castrated Attis, the mythic original of the *galli*, has left his mark on the scene. Indeed, it is as if the Virgilian Cybele could not but bring the Catullan Attis in her train: the copious hexameter devoted to Cybele's progeny, *omnis caelicolas, omnis supera alta tenentis*, literally incorporates (and, to the ear, exactly echoes) the opening words of the long poem Catullus devoted to Attis: *Super alta* (63.1).[71] Another still more inapposite Catullan intertext presses upon the description of Cybele "embracing a hundred descendants," *centum complexa nepotes*. *Nepos* is a perfectly good word for "descendant," used regularly in that sense (or the more limited "grandchild") throughout the epic. But in less elevated contexts *nepos* can mean "playboy," an inadmissible sense in this passage, of course, albeit one that *complexa* may bring halfway to mind. The inappropriate passage that resonates here is Catullus' fierce farewell to Lesbia, a poem that likewise conjoins a hyperbolic tour of a world conquered, or imagined conquerable, by the might of a Caesar (*Caesaris ... magni*, 11.10) with the image of a woman "embracing" an impossible number of men (17–20):[72]

> cum suis vivat valeatque moechis,
> quos simul complexa tenet trecentos,
> nullum amans vere, sed identidem omnium
>     ilia rumpens.

[69] See Wiseman (1984) on Virgil's contribution to the "Augustan rehabilitation" of Cybele, Augustus' neighbor (along with Victory and Actian Apollo) on the Palatine.

[70] For details, see Wiseman (1984).

[71] Putnam (1989) 29 n. 4.

[72] And in each case, the imperial survey includes line-final *Indos* (Catull. 11.2, Virg. *Aen.* 6.794) and *Nilus/Nili* (Catull. 11.8, Virg. *Aen.* 6.800); see Putnam (1989).

> Let her live and fare well with her playboys, whom she holds and hugs three hundred at a time, loving none of them really, but over and over again breaking the groins of them all.

It has long been recognized that Catullus puts Roman imperial expansion, the burden of the opening stanzas of this poem, into problematic dialogue with his mistress's rapacious sexual appetite. In effect, the Virgilian passage comes up against the same conjunction, but from the other side.

I am not proposing that Virgil means to equate Cybele-Roma with Catullus' promiscuous Lesbia.[73] I would even entertain the possibility that these Catullan echoes are unauthorized, a form of interference issuing not from the poet's self-consciousness but from the textual unconscious, constituting an unwitting commentary by the later poet on the earlier one. Yet even if not meant, the echoes are still meaningful. The burden they bear is the surplus of ambivalence that attends the image of the mother, even the divine mother (of) Rome herself.[74] The fecund mother may rejoice in her abundance of virile sons, but her imperial potency seems always to carry the threat of their impairment.

---

[73] Still less that the "allusion" participates in a subterranean current of anti-Augustanism; fecundity and desire are core values of Roman imperialism, as Virgil knows, and as Ovid will insist.

[74] Cf. Panoussi (2003) 124.

# CHAPTER

# 3

# Variations on a phallic theme

The previous chapter brought me to the verge; now I close my eyes and step right over, taking the plunge into one of the most embarrassing and rebarbative of psychoanalytic obsessions: the Freudian penis, the Lacanian phallus.

There is no way around the fact that this is a pivotal topic in classical psychoanalytic theory. For Freud, it is the penis that signposts the devious journey that arrives, with surprising frequency, and as if by design, at normative heterosexuality.[1] Fear of losing it ("castration anxiety") spurs the son to relinquish the mother; wanting it ("penis envy") sets the girl on the winding path toward motherhood, which alone can abate her sense of privation.[2] In one of Freud's everyday myths, the differentiating crisis is triggered by the sight of a different body, perceived as fearfully deficient or enviably furnished. Whereas the boy's reaction has to be activated by a threat of castration (it is only in tandem with this threat that the girl's body appears castrated, thereby furnishing ghastly proof that such threats are not always empty), the girl's is instantaneous: "she has seen it and knows that she is without it and wants to have it."[3] Though sometimes refusing the evidence of his eyes, the Freudian boy typically has the good sense to relinquish his

---

[1] The perspective of Freud (1905), e.g., "Every step on this long path of development can become a point of fixation, every juncture in this involved combination can be an occasion for a dissociation of the sexual instinct" (235).

[2] See, respectively, Freud (1924) and Freud (1925).

[3] Freud (1925) 252. The notorious contrast is nuanced elsewhere; see Mitchell (1982) 17.

mother in order to keep his penis. By contrast, the Freudian girl scarcely ever succeeds in recovering fully from her initial disappointment. And the consequences of this difference ramify far beyond individual sexual destinies. The catastrophic destruction of the boy's Oedipus complex precipitates his transformation into a moral and social being, newly equipped with a conscience (the super-ego, created via the introjection of the forbidding father) and enhanced social connections (the effect of sublimation). But penis envy only sets the stage for the girl's oedipal phase, something from which she will emerge only gradually if ever, and the installation of her super-ego will likewise be a gradual and tentative affair. Hence Freud's notorious observation that "for women the level of what is ethically normal is different from what it is in men. Their super-ego is never so inexorable, so impersonal, so independent of its emotional origins as we require it to be in men."[4]

Lacan is more evenhanded and more abstract, hence potentially less objectionable than Freud. For Lacan, the phallus is not a body-part but the representation of what everybody is without. Everyone is "castrated" in that being a subject means being subjected to signification: divided and displaced from any supposed center of meaning, caught in a web of names one did not spin. In Lacan's playful rewriting of the Freudian scene, the emphasis accordingly shifts from the body to language. Instead of reacting to the sight of each other's bodies, Lacan's little boy and girl, discovered sitting opposite each other on a train as it pulls into a station, look out the window and read the signs: "'Look,' says the brother, 'we're at Ladies!' 'Imbecile!' replies his sister, 'Don't you see we're at Gentlemen.'" It is from the other that each receives word of his or her destiny: "To these children, Gentlemen and Ladies will henceforth be two homelands toward which each of their souls will take flight on divergent wings." These two homelands being "in fact the same homeland," as Lacan observes, sexual difference appears to be nothing more than an effect of signification.[5]

Even so, law-abiding human subjects past a certain age must pass through just one of those doors, under just one of those signs. The interpellation of the doors may not reflect a real difference, but it does produce one, and this difference, though arbitrary, is nonetheless absolute. Moreover, the arbitrariness has its limits. After all, the signifier of

[4] Freud (1925) 257.    [5] Lacan ([1957] 2006) 417.

93

signifiers is not just *any* symbol. As many critics have pointed out, the phallus never quite severs its ties with its humble fleshly partner.[6] All subjects may be castrated, but some seem to be more castrated than others. Every child has to make the dreadful discovery that the phallic mother lacks a phallus (according to Lacan, this discovery is what really tightens the screw of the castration complex), but no such revelation awaits when it comes to the "phallic father." Thus if anatomy is not destiny, it determines feminine and masculine positions almost as if it were: women lack, men have, not the phallus (no one does) but its organic approximation – and this appears to make all the difference. For Lacan as for Freud, then, sexed subjects are determined by their relation to one thing, the virile thing.

Freud's contemporaries were quick to raise objections to this "phallocentric" scheme (as Ernest Jones was already terming it in 1927). As Karen Horney remarked, the whole theory sounds like a projection of a little boy's "typical ideas" of feminine anatomy.[7] More recently, the most significant challenges have come from the side of cultural history. Sander Gilman, for example, has placed Freud's castrated woman squarely within the contemporary problematics of the "castrated" (circumcised) Jew, while Gary Taylor has shown his eccentric emphasis on the penis – as opposed to the testicles, the normal target of castration – to be both an effect and an index of a larger cultural shift in the meaning of sexuality, from reproduction to pleasure.[8] To the extent that he remains in the abstract zone of signification, Lacan seems to advance a more viably universal theory. Still, insofar as the Lacanian phallus yields some of the same results as the Freudian penis (penis envy and castration anxiety, later absorbed under the rubric of "mourning the phallus"), the theory is open to the same objections.[9]

Freud's champions often make the point, and it is a good one, that his critics only beg the question by naturalizing the very phenomena (sexual difference, normative heterosexuality) that Freud set out to explain. For

[6] See, most provocatively, Butler (1993) 73–91 and (re Ovid's Tiresias) Liveley (2003). Lacan is not blind to the penile residuum, of course; see, e.g., Lacan ([1958] 2006) 576.

[7] Jones (1927) (proposing "aphanisis" in place of "castration"); Horney ([1926] 1967).

[8] Gilman (1995) (e.g., 36–40); Taylor (2000) 85–109.

[9] Castration complex: Lacan ([1958] 2006) 576, 582; "mourning the phallus": Lacan ([1959] 1982).

Horney as for Jones, it is self-evident that girls are born girls, and born heterosexual; sexual maturation is the realization of a nature that is already given. For Freud as for Lacan, sexed bodies are born, but boys and girls are made; the question is how. I confess to finding their minimalist answer (requiring nothing more than a simple on/off toggle switch, as it were) quite elegant. Yet I feel no impulse, much less obligation, to maintain that it is correct. My readings in this chapter are not meant to bolster psychoanalytic theory by discovering confirmatory "cases" of penis envy and castration anxiety. (One might argue, to the contrary, that the stories told by Freud and Lacan themselves derive from and effectively continue the fictions of antiquity.) Penis envy and castration anxiety furnish the terrain of this chapter, not its destination.

The focus of my first section is the workings of the textual unconscious in an Ovidian story about a woman's desire. Finding "phallic symbols" in Ovid's poetry does not pose much of a challenge, and if I indulge in that old-fashioned pastime here, it is for the sake of the textual network the roving phallus helps me stitch together. In my second section, I return to Catullus and experiment with pushing the symptomatic reading to its limits, tracking the intermittent effects of castration anxiety across the long poems. This is the section in which I am both most aware of the gaps between Freudian and Roman models of sexuality and most doctrinaire in my deployment of Freudian schemes – a combination that reflects the unresolved blend of detachment and engagement that informs my relation to psychoanalysis.

## What Scylla wants: phallic figurations in Ovid's *Metamorphoses*

*Metamorphoses* 8 opens with the story of a girl in love. In many ways it is a simple story, a variation on the classic theme of desire vs. duty. Like many a heroine before her – one thinks especially of the young Medea of *Metamorphoses* 7 – Scylla is smitten with a stranger and, after a brief tussle with her conscience, betrays her fatherland in the hope of winning his love. What makes the story interesting for my purposes is the way other desires, not just unconfessed but seemingly unrecognized by Scylla, announce themselves along the way. The text communicates with us, as it were, behind Scylla's back. It sprouts local parapraxes and symptomatic repetitions to which she has no access, and it inserts her story into a larger poetic structure that she has no opportunity to read.

Of course, works of literature typically involve some such imbalance of knowledge, with the characters, no matter how self-conscious they may be, always outfoxed to some extent by the encompassing design (one that even the author may not perfectly control). In many cases, this imbalance is a trivial side-effect of traditional thematic patterning; it is true, for example, but hardly worth remarking, that Virgil's Dido is unaware that her suicide literalizes the poet's earlier language of erotic "wound" and "fire." At times, though, the text's "knowing more" can produce an effect of the character's "knowing less," whether because the knowledge has been repressed (as seems the case with the guiltily mourning Orpheus of *Metamorphoses* 10), or because it is structurally unavailable, part of an impersonal, intertextual unconscious (Ascanius does not himself "identify with" Pentheus).[10] Though one might be tempted to supply Scylla with a personal unconscious, in the event the episode will not so much disclose what Scylla "really" wants as spin out the network of associations that feed into her desire.

This Scylla is not the notorious girl-turned-sea-monster whose trans-formation will be described later in the poem, but Scylla the daughter of King Nisus of Megara. (The homonymy enrolls the monster in the textual unconscious of this episode; as we will see, the one Scylla cannot but take on board some of the other's distinctive traits.) The story begins with two fathers at war. En route to Athens with an army to avenge the death of his son, Minos of Crete decides to test his battle-strength first by laying siege to Megara. The first thing we learn about his opposite number, the king of Megara, is that he has a talismanic lock of purple hair clinging to the top of his white head (the contrasting colors are picked out by line-final *ostro* "purple" and *canos* "white" at 8.8–9), a lock which is "the guarantee of his great kingdom" (*magni fiducia regni*, 10). Misbegotten passion finds its way into the story during the ensuing conflict, when "the fortunes of war hung suspended, and Victory long flew between the two sides on undecided wings" (*pendebat adhuc belli fortuna, diuque | inter utrumque volat dubiis Victoria pennis*,

---

[10] See above, 19–25 and 69–70.

12–13), giving Scylla plenty of time to admire, with increasing energy, the handsome enemy commander. To win his favor, she resolves to clip her father's purple lock and to deliver it, and with it, her father and his city, into her beloved's hands. Instead of embracing his benefactress, however, Minos is appalled by her act of treachery, spurns her as the most vicious of monsters, and speedily sets sail for Crete. The abandoned Scylla leaps after the ship and miraculously succeeds in clinging to the stern, until her vengeful father (transformed meanwhile, Ovid parenthetically informs us, into a sea-hawk) swoops down to break her hold. As she falls away from the ship, Scylla is likewise transformed into a bird, the *ciris* or "cleaver." The avian implications of purple-crested Nisus, hovering fortune, and winged Victory at the beginning of the episode are thus made good in the double bird transformation at its conclusion; this is the metamorphic frame that guarantees the story a place within Ovid's poem of changes.

Scylla presents the profile of a classically Freudian female, one endowed with the sketchiest of super-egos. The initial soliloquy in which she puzzles through her options is checked by just one fleeting moral qualm. What felicity, she imagines, to fly to the Cretan encampment, confess her love to King Minos, and ask "what dowry he would be willing to be bought for" (*qua dote ... vellet emi*, 8.53–4). There is just one price she *will not* pay (54–6):

> tantum patrias ne posceret arces!
> nam pereant potius sperata cubilia, quam sim
> proditione potens –

Only let him not demand my father's citadel! I'd sooner lose the marriage bed I desire than win it by treachery –

Yet the moral revulsion, marked by the sputtering p's, doesn't even last out the hexameter. No sooner is the forbidden impulse given voice than the bar that enables it to surface, in this comically token instance of negation, begins to rise, like a semaphore at a train-crossing: " – and yet the clemency of a mild conqueror has often rendered defeat a benefit to the defeated" (*quamvis saepe utile vinci* / *victoris placidi fecit clementia victis*, 56–7). Once reason has joined forces with desire, the father comes to appear merely as an extension of the locked gates that represent his conventional function, which is to block and obstruct: "The bolts of the city gates are in my father's keeping; he's the only one I fear, alas; he alone hinders my hopes" (*claustraque portarum genitor tenet; hunc ego solum / infelix timeo, solus mea vota moratur*, 70–1). And having identified the obstacle, Scylla baldly, boldly wishes it away: "Would to god I were fatherless!" (*di facerent sine patre forem!*, 72). Ever alert for its opportunities, her desire picks up on the conventional formula and generates a supplementary philosophical argument: "Everyone is his own god, that's certain" (*sibi quisque profecto / est deus*, 72–3). Viewed in that light, her tardiness appears to be nothing less than shameful: another woman in her plight would long since have taken the initiative and done away with "whatever stood in the way of her love" (*quodcumque obstaret amori*, 75). And as the ensuing rush of verbs suggests (*intrat, spoliat, pervenit*, 85–9, dominating their respective hexameters), Scylla will proceed to dispatch the prohibiting paternal "whatever" without hesitation or the least sign of distress.

And yet, though Scylla has little feeling to spare for her own father, the paradox of this episode is that the man by whom she is obsessed is himself a preeminently fatherly figure. Ovid's readers will have encountered Minos already in *Metamorphoses* 7, where he was discovered preparing to wage war against Athens, relying not only on his fine army and fleet but also and especially, Ovid tells us, on his "fatherly anger" (*patria tamen est firmissimus ira*, 7.457). This is the righteous anger he feels as a father bereaved of a child (his son Androgeos, who met his death in Attica). But the phrase also hints at Minos' traditional character as the super-father, the very model of paternal severity, destined to sit in judgment on errant souls in the underworld. It is in just this character that Minos appears when he condemns Scylla as the "scandal of the age" (8.97) and a veritable "monster" (100) of filial impiety. Morally at least, the one father sides with the other. And Nisus will subsequently return the favor by rescuing Minos' ship from Scylla's clutches. The intervention, the more striking because it is his only action in the episode, turns Nisus into the emblem of paternal wrath he was destined to become: the punitive father-bird forever pursuing the guilty daughter-bird.[11] For all that they are at war with each other, then, the two fathers are as one in their hostility to Scylla.

[11] So they appear in Virg. *Geo.* 1.404–9.

It turns out that the father is never marginal to Scylla's story; he is always there, whatever name he bears. He is there, moreover, not only as a figure of prohibition and punitive rage, but also as an object of desire. Committed in the dead of night, in her father's very bedchamber (*thalamos ... paternos*, 8.84), Scylla's filial trespass reads very much as an incestuous adventure (one thinks especially of Ovid's Myrrha, upcoming in *Metamorphoses* 10); there is even a standard-issue immorality-abetting "nurse" on hand, albeit in this case a figurative one, "night the greatest nurturer of erotic cares" (*curarum maxima nutrix / nox*, 81–2), to abet the timid virgin's crime.[12] The innuendo may seem inevitable (where and when else could Scylla commit her crime?), but it is also symptomatic. From the very outset, Scylla seems to confound the fatherly figure she adores with the father whose existence she acknowledges only as a hindrance to her desires. As Ovid writes it, her infatuation with Minos focuses on his head, first covered (8.24–6) –

> hac iudice Minos
> seu caput abdiderat cristata casside pennis,
> in galea formosus erat

did Minos have his head hidden by a feather-crested helm, she thought him lovely in a helmet

– and finally (after due celebration of the warrior's beauty when set off by shield, spear, and bow) exposed (32–6):

> cum vero faciem dempto nudaverat aere
> purpureusque albi stratis insignia pictis
> terga premebat equi spumantiaque ora regebat,
> vix sua, vix sanae virgo Niseia compos
> mentis erat.

but when, bronze [helmet] doffed, he had bared his countenance, and rode purple on a white horse's back decked with tapestries, reining around its frothing mouth, then was the maiden daughter of Nisus hardly in command of herself, hardly in her right mind.

---

[12] The incestuous note is amplified by the *Ciris* poet, who has an actual *nutrix*, finding Scylla approaching her father's bedroom, worry that she may be afflicted with the same passion as Myrrha! For a different take on the intertextual implications, see Knox (1990).

Either way, when Scylla looks at Minos, it is as if she were seeing Nisus. The helmeted head with its feathery crest conjures up the image of the distinctively tufted king (both before and after his avian transformation). But it is when Minos "bares his countenance" that the father really comes into focus; it is at this moment that the text dangles before our eyes Nisus' signature colors, purple and white, *purpureusque albi*.[13] The association is ungrammatical; the adjectives attach not to Minos' head but to his royally "purple" cloak (one presumes) and "white" charger. Yet the conjunction of the helmet's removal with the sudden promotion of this color contrast has the effect of a revelation, albeit a revelation made despite the superficial grammar, or opportunistically by way of it. It is such details, available to the reader who reads, but unavailable to the character who sees, or even to the narrator who relates, that produce the unconsciousness-effect of the text.

The fusion of Minos and Nisus is consummated, again through a textual figure that exceeds Scylla's intentions, at the moment that Scylla sets out to exchange the one for the other. Having despoiled her father of the fateful lock (*fatali nata parentem | crine suum spoliat*, 8.85–6), the princess charges through the enemy camp until she reaches Minos (89–94):

> quem sic adfata paventem est:
> "suasit amor facinus; proles ego regia Nisi
> Scylla tibi trado patriaeque meosque Penates.
> praemia nulla peto nisi te; cape pignus amoris
> purpureum crinem nec me nunc tradere crinem,
> sed patrium tibi crede caput."

whom trembling before her thus she addressed: "Love swayed me to do the deed; I, royal offspring of Nisus, Scylla, hand over to you my fatherland's and my own household gods. I seek no reward but you; take this pledge of my love, the purple lock, nor think it a lock I now put into your hands, but my father's very head."

---

[13] The detail is noticed by Tsitsiou-Chelidoni in the course of her rich discussion of the episode, one that approaches many of the same issues I address (e.g., Scylla's restricted knowledge of textual effects such as this) from the perspective of narratology; see Tsitsiou-Chelidoni (2003) 35–117, in particular 52–3 (on the paternal color-contrast) and 63–85 (on the virtuoso immorality of Scylla's soliloquy).

The convergence of fathers is underwritten by the bizarre description of Minos as *paventem* ("trembling"); change one letter, and Scylla is addressing her "parent" (compare line-final *parentem* just a few lines earlier, 85). And in Scylla's bold "I seek no reward but you," the words "but you," *nisi te*, literally attach the paternal name to the beloved object – an astonishing parapraxis, rendered the more noticeable by the proximity of *Nisi* ( = "of Nisus"), which fell from Scylla's lips just two lines earlier.[14] What Scylla wants, it seems, is not so much Minos as the father for whom he stands.

It is always satisfying to uncover a suppressed narrative of incest. Yet incest is not the end of Scylla's story. The most fundamental and most troublesome desire uncovered by this episode is not Scylla's desire for Minos, nor even her desire for Nisus, but Scylla's desire to be her father, or more abstractly, and in this case I believe more accurately, Scylla's desire for the phallus: penis envy, or better (because more encompassing), phallus envy. It may be that her infatuation with Minos is a defensive ruse designed to palliate the guilt of this desire.[15] After all, as Scylla angrily reminds the Cretan king as he sails away from Megara, her crime against Nisus was committed as a service to Minos; she took the lock for his sake, not her own; she took it only in order to surrender it – not to keep it. This is what Scylla says; it may be what we are meant to believe that she believes. But the text keeps telling us something different.

One of the most striking features of this episode is Scylla's reiterated appropriation, in mimic form, of a masculine identity. This impulse is evident in her soliloquy, which rehearses, with dazzling glibness, the virile discourses of the deliberating senator ("The enterprise has my vote, my resolution is taken," 8.67), the sententious philosopher ("Fortune spurns the prayers of idlers!" 73), and the bold soldier ("Why should any woman outbrave me? Through fire, through steel I'd venture!" 76–7). It also shapes the narrator's preamble to her incessant admiration of Minos, *hac iudice Minos* (24), literally "with this [girl] as judge, Minos" (was beautiful whatever he wore or did). The sentiment may be an amatory commonplace, yet what the juxtaposition seems to

---

[14] I owe this observation to Justin Schwab. The difference of vowel quantity may temper the effect but does not erase it.

[15] A famous account of this strategy in Riviere ([1929] 1986). For a complementary discussion of Ovid's Salmacis, see Nugent (1990).

communicate, alongside Scylla's adoration of Minos, is her desire to usurp the judicial position that by rights belongs to him. In the form of hostile emulation, the same impulse contours Scylla's first appearance in the poem, atop the royal tower with its famously resonant walls (*vocalibus … muris*, 14), walls "upon which Leto's son is said to have set down his golden lyre; its sound clung to the stone" (*in quibus auratam proles Letoia fertur | deposuisse lyram; saxo sonus eius inhaesit*, 15–16). Tourists in Pausanias' day still threw pebbles at the walls of Megara to elicit an echo of Apollo's lyre (Paus. 1.42.2), and Ovid's Scylla is likewise in the habit of entertaining herself by "attacking" the massive mural stones with a diminutive pebble (*saepe illuc solita est ascendere filia Nisi | et petere exiguo resonantia saxa lapillo*, 17–18). The Apollonian *sonus* in the tower walls resembles the city's other outstanding feature, the other guarantee of its stability: the lock of hair that was described as "clinging to" the top of the king's head a few lines earlier (*inhaerebat*, 10). Endowed with the god's own voice, the resounding tower is the object both of Scylla's aggression and of her desire, the mirror of an ideal and unachievable self.

Scylla's most effective appropriation of a masculine position comes with her assault on her father, an act of heroism that gains particular point when set against the story of Jason and Medea in *Metamorphoses* 7. When Scylla reproaches herself for falling short of the standard of boldness set by "another girl afire with such a passion" (*altera … succensa cupidine tanto*, 8.74), it is Medea who comes to mind. And when she describes her father's lock as "more precious than gold" (*auro pretiosior*, 79), the proverbial comparison may conjure up the image of the golden fleece (termed simply *auro*, 7.155) that Jason carried off with Medea's help in the previous book. Yet Scylla's role model is finally less Medea than Jason. As he "takes possession of the gold" (*auro … potitur*, 7.155–6) and carries off as "spoils" both fleece and Medea (*spolio*, 156; *spolia*, 157), so Scylla "despoils her father of his lock" and "tak[es] possession of her wicked prize" (*parentem | crine suum spoliat praedaque potita nefanda*, 8.85–6), hoping thereby to win another prize in the form of Minos.[16] Everything takes place as if Scylla had read the previous book and were intent on correcting Ovid's and/or Jason's masculinist

---

[16] The parallel is still closer if we deviate from Tarrant to admit 8.87 (*fert secum spolium sceleris*, cf. *muneris auctorem secum, spolia altera, portans* at 7.157). The

bias by reclaiming the heroic role for the woman in the story. But Scylla has not read it, and she does not have access to the textual particulars that confirm her connection to both Medea and Jason. Here as elsewhere, it is the material text that gives us access to desires that remain unrecognized and unexpressed.

Scylla's virile ambitions have interesting consequences for her representation of Minos. In her soliloquy, as we have seen, she is already scheming to "buy" Minos with an appropriate "dowry"; and though her original impulse was to "hand over" to Minos both herself and her fatherland (*tradere mecum / dotalem patriam*, 8.67–8), the purchase price she finally settles on includes her fatherland and her father's "head" but not herself. In this perverse transaction, it is the fathers who are exchanged, the daughter who controls the exchange. This reversal helps determine Minos' attitude when Scylla addresses herself to him (*quem sic adfata paventem est*, 89). That *paventem* is a strange way of describing the stern warlord is confirmed by the palliating translations generally on offer ("startled," "horrified"), which seem designed to smooth over the indecorous scenario of King Minos trembling before a mere chit of a girl. But the text is here as elsewhere complicit with its heroine: the emasculation of the father finds an echo in the fearful posture of Minos before Scylla, purple lock in hand.

In fact the inversion of gender protocols is a pervasive feature of this episode, with patronymics and matronymics operating according to a principle of cross-gendering, son being identified through mother, daughter through father. The recurrence of the father's name in connection with Scylla (termed variously "daughter of Nisus," "Niseian maiden," and, most grandly, in her own formula, "royal offspring of Nisus") may seem unexceptional.[17] But the patronymic gains point when juxtaposed with Minos' matronymic, which surfaces, and not by chance, in an early passage focalized through Scylla: she has learned to recognize the names and accoutrements of all the principal enemy warriors, and above all, we are told, "the countenance of their general, Europa's son" (*faciem ducis Europaei*, 8.23). The implications of this matronymic are subsequently unfolded in the soliloquizing Scylla's very oddly formulated appreciation of her beloved's beauty: "If the woman

emphasis on *spolia* may also activate the etymology of "Scylla" qua ship-"ravager"; see Tsitsiou-Chelidoni (2003) 91–2.

[17] 8.17, 35, 90; conversely, Apollo enters as *proles Letoia* (8.15).

who bore you, fairest of creatures, was such a beauty as you are, the god had good reason to burn for her" (*si quae te peperit talis, pulcherrime rerum, / qualis es, ipsa fuit, merito deus arsit in illa*, 49–50). One might have expected Scylla to liken Minos to his father Jupiter, the ultimate lady-killer. Instead, what she sees (or imagines) when she looks at Minos is his resemblance to his mother, the beautiful object of divine desire. Her patronizing appreciation of Minos' feminine beauty puts Scylla in the role of the passionate and omnipotent king of Olympus. So too, perhaps, with her patronymic, which may signal not only her subordinate status as a derivative of her father's identity, but also her desire to stand for her father and in his place.

It is typical of Ovid that the authority of the father does not remain untarnished across this episode. Not even he owns the phallus; he too is subject to, spoken by, the signifiers he thinks he controls. The severity with which Minos spurns Scylla's advances, trampling her hopes of accompanying him home – "I will not suffer the cradle of Jupiter, Crete, which is my sphere, to be tainted by such a monster as you!" (8.99–100) – is very evidently fueled by the energy of a projection, since (as everybody knows) the Crete Minos is determined to keep pure is already tainted by the presence of the quintessentially monstrous Minotaur. All the same, Scylla seems to take the charge to heart. The accusations with which she in turn loads Minos' departing ship are entirely conventional, save for one detail: "it wasn't Europa who bore you, no, it was the inhospitable Syrtis – Armenian tigresses – wind-churned Charybdis!" (120–1). What is missing here (replaced by another disyllabic "S" name) is the traditional partner of Charybdis: the other Scylla, the literal monster who has already put in an appearance, coupled with Charybdis as usual, a book earlier (7.63–5), though her transformation will not be recounted until much later in the poem (via an etiological flashback triggered by *Met.* 13.730ff.). It is as if Minos' accusation had unearthed this lurking association, which Scylla now attempts to bury anew by projecting monstrosity back onto her accuser: his father, she taunts, was not Jupiter disguised as a bull, but a real bull (*verus / qui te progenuit taurus fuit*, 8.123, 125), making him the perfect husband for Pasiphae, mother of the Minotaur. It is this bastard, now embarrassingly full grown, that greets Minos on his return to Crete. Though he hastens to hide the monster away in the labyrinth, the suppressed Minotaur (never so named) peeks out in the description of the grateful hecatomb the victorious Minos offers to his father Jove, *vota **Iovi Minos taurorum** corpora centum / solvit* (152–3), a formulation that catches Minos between his two affiliations, divine and bestial. Like his homeland of Crete, Minos is himself infected by the monstrosity he abhors.

There are other pressures that help contour Minos' harshly worded rejection of Scylla (8.97–100):

> di te submoveant, o nostri infamia saecli,
> orbe suo, tellusque tibi pontusque negetur.
> certe ego non patiar Iovis incunabula, Creten,
> qui meus est orbis, tantum contingere monstrum.

May the gods banish you, you scandal of our age, from their sphere, and may land and sea be denied you! Certainly I will not suffer Jove's cradle, Crete, which is my sphere, to be tainted by such a monster!

The focus on "spheres" helps flag the connection with the upcoming story of Daedalus, maker of the labyrinth, to whom Minos will likewise deny access to land and sea (like Scylla and her father, Daedalus and his son will end up taking to the air). But the reiterated *orbis* also has work to do in its immediate context. The reason Minos is at war is that his own "cradle" has been robbed of a son; the reiterated *orbis* marks the place of the unspoken word that identifies the king's condition: *orbus*, "bereaved." In this tangle of grief and rage, Scylla serves as a reminder of the surviving, monstrous child who has taken Androgeos' place in Crete. A subsequent play on *orbis/orbus* suggests that Scylla has unwittingly received the unspoken message. No place will give her shelter, she complains: "I am exposed, bereft of lands," *exponimur orbae / terrarum* (117–18; the startling *orbae terrarum* distorts the idiomatic *orbis terrarum*, "the world").[18] The adjective, which suits an orphaned child as well as a bereaved parent, complements *exponere*, the *vox propria* for the "exposure" of unwanted offspring; it is as if Scylla were experiencing her

---

[18] The text is much disputed. The manuscripts offer *obstruximus orbem* (which Tarrant prints) as well as *exponimur orbe*, which (with Bentley's minimal emendation of *orbe* to *orbae*) Anderson adopts and I prefer; see further Anderson (1972) 345–6. Though producing its own problems, this reading gives point to the (otherwise flabby) enjambed *terrarum* as a self-censoring correction (the parricidal Scylla can hardly have the face to describe herself as "bereft").

abandonment by Minos as, in effect, his belated "exposure" of an unwanted child (so Minos, back in Crete, will lock away another intensely unwanted child, exposure not being feasible in this instance). Preserved from a hostile father in his Cretan cradle, baby Jupiter will grow up to castrate and replace that father. Is Jupiter, here likewise, a model for the daughter of Nisus?

If what Scylla wants is the father's phallus, she is doomed never to have it. The conclusion to the Ovidian story of Scylla is not the traditional one, which features a punitive Minos tying Scylla to his ship and dragging her through the water to her death, from which she is rescued by her transformation into a bird. In Ovid's surreal variation, it is Scylla who attaches herself to the ship, longing to be "dragged," determined not to be left behind (8.141–4):

> "insequar invitum puppemque amplexa recurvam
> per freta longa trahar." vix dixerat, insilit undis
> consequiturque rates faciente cupidine vires
> Cnosiacaeque haeret comes invidiosa carinae.

"Like it or not, I'll come after you, I'll clasp the curving poop and be dragged across the long stretch of sea." Scarcely was she done speaking, when she leaps into the water, overtakes the ships (desire affords her the strength) and clings, a hateful escort, to the Cretan hull.

This is Scylla at her most monstrous, Scylla the fit partner of Charybdis.[19] Even so, her grip is broken by her father, who swoops down "to tear her with hooked beak as she clung" (*ut haerentem rostro laceraret adunco*, 147), precipitating the transformation with which the episode concludes.

The passage is the culmination of a series of references to the parts of ships, in particular to the stern or poop, *puppis*, and the keel, *carina*. These are common synecdoches for "ship" in Latin poetry, of course. Still, the clustering draws attention to them. It might even make us hesitate over the meaning of the just-cited "hooked beak," *rostro*: bird's

---

[19] Cf. Medea's fantasy of sailing with Jason past Charybdis and Scylla (!): "clinging [*haerens*] to Jason's breast will I be borne across the long stretch of sea" (*per freta longa ferar*, 7.66–7); Medea will turn out to be a monster in her own right, of course.

beak, or ship's beak? The story begins with a special part, the *purpureus crinis*, as Scylla describes it to Minos at line 93, and all parts point back to that part, *the* part. We may detect its traces in a pair of line-endings, as the departing Minos orders rowers to man the "poops," *impelli remige puppes* (103), and Scylla sees the sea afloat with "keels," *nare carinas* (104).[20] Certainly it helps shape the description of Scylla "clinging" to the "keel" of Minos' ship, *haeret ... carinae*, as the lock is described "clinging" to Nisus' head at the very beginning of the episode, *crinis inhaerebat* (10). It is a fine stroke of poetic justice to have Nisus detach Scylla from the *carina*: he does to her what she did to him. (That the episode has come full circle is underscored by the overarching chiasmus linking lines 10 and 144: *crinis inhaerebat ... haeret comes invidiosa carinae*.) But Scylla is not castrated. She is herself in the place of the part which is cut off from the whole. Scylla's fate, and for Freud and Lacan this is every woman's fate, is not to have but to be the phallus. Her claim to it – her intermittently betrayed conviction that she does after all already have it (a feature of feminine psychology on which Freud commented with some bemusement) – is accordingly countered by the most literal possible enactment of what it means, properly speaking, to be a woman. By cutting her off with his hooked beak and sending her into flight, Nisus enacts his own recuperation of the masculine position as well as, and by way of, Scylla's permanent dispossession. The etymology that seals the Ovidian episode yields a similar conclusion: "transformed into a bird, she is called Ciris, a name she got from the shorn lock" (*in avem mutata vocatur / Ciris et a tonso est hoc nomen adepta capillo*, 150–1). The bird name derives from the Greek verb κείρω ("cut, shear"), which is represented here by its Latin equivalent: *Ciris ... a tonso* (from *tondeo*). But there may be a secondary, less pointed, Latin etymology lurking in the final word of the episode, *capillo*, "hair": one word for "lock of hair" in Latin is *cirrus*. The doubleness would fit: Scylla is both the cutter and the lock.

The term "phallus," which gets a lot of play in contemporary psychoanalytic discourse, does not carry the same transgressive charge in a

---

[20] The association is overdetermined by the phallic potential of the ship; see, e.g., Ovid *Ars* 3.748 (*ut tangat portus fessa carina suos*) with Gibson (2003) 381.

culture in which the phallus is regularly on display. Though the Roman sense of decency kept the literal penis under wraps,[21] the Roman commitment to power kept the symbolic phallus very much in the public eye: in garden statues and wall paintings of Priapus, on monuments and paving stones, in the protective amulets boys wore around their necks, slung under the chariots of triumphing generals, and even, if we believe Barbara Kellum, designed into the ground plan of the Forum of Augustus.[22] Under such circumstances, "phallic symbolism" is not a dark secret unveiled by the labors of the prying critic but part of the surface texture of the story that is being told. Though epic decorum may sever it from its genital base, the phallus only circulates the more energetically in the various virile excrescences that stand ready to transport it through the Ovidian narrative.

The figurative equivalence of these excrescences helps organize the phallic comedy of which Scylla's comeuppance forms, in the event, but the first act. The book that opens with Scylla cutting off her father's purple lock (and that showcases Meleager, another hero whose life is bound up with a phallic talisman) ends with the river god Achelous loudly lamenting the loss of one of his horns.[23] The scene is the dinner party at which Achelous is entertaining a company of heroes heading home from the Caledonian boar hunt. In the book's closing lines, Achelous, who has just finished telling the story of Erysichthon and his shape-shifting daughter, bethinks himself of his own metamorphic abilities. He too is a shape-shifter, sometimes appearing as a river god, sometimes as a snake, while sometimes, he boasts, "I'm lord of the herd and gather my strength into my horns" (*armenti modo dux vires in cornua sumo*, 8.882). But the mention of "horns" pulls him up short (883–4): "'Horns, while I could! Now half my brow lacks its weapon, as you yourself can see'; groans accompanied his words" (*"cornua, dum potui. nunc pars caret altera telo / frontis, ut ipse vides." gemitus sunt verba secuti*, 883–4). So ends the book of Scylla; the next book opens with Theseus asking for, and Achelous supplying, the story behind his mutilated brow: it was battling with Hercules for the

[21] See Hallett (2005) 61–101 on Roman attitudes to real-life nudity (degrading), a strong contrast to their eventual embrace of nudity in art (ennobling, heroic, deific, etc.).

[22] Kellum (1996).

[23] On the linkage of lock, log, and horn, see Crabbe (1981) 2287, 2301–2.

hand of Deianeira, we learn, that cost him his horn. It is this missing horn that frames this first episode of *Metamorphoses* 9, with *truncae ... frontis* at the start (1–2), and *trunca ... fronte* again just before the close (86).

This tale of phallic injuries reaches a kind of resolution at the end of *Metamorphoses* 9, in the story of Iphis: a story with a marvelously happy ending, and one that positively abounds in horns. When pregnant, Iphis' mother is visited by the goddess Isis, who instructs her to defy her husband's orders and raise her child, even if it is (as of course it will be) a girl. The first detail Ovid singles out in his description of Isis, who is identified here with the bovine Io (*Inachis*, 9.687), is the set of "lunar horns" on her brow (*inerant lunaria fronti / cornua*, 688–9; the war at Megara was likewise dated by the "moon's horns," *cornua lunae*, 8.11). The mother obeys the goddess and raises her daughter as a boy, concealing her true sex from all the world. All goes well until Iphis falls in love with another girl, to whom she is eventually betrothed by her unsuspecting father. When the day of the marriage can no longer be put off, her mother offers a desperate prayer to Isis, "goddess of the seven-horned Nile" (*septem digestum in cornua Nilum*, 774).[24] At the end of the previous book, the words of Achelous were accompanied by groans (*gemitus sunt verba secuti*, 8.884); at the end of this one, the words of Iphis' mother are accompanied by tears (*lacrimae sunt verba secutae*, 9.781; these are the only such locutions in the poem), and to happier effect: her moon-like horns gleaming (783–4), Isis signals her assent, and Iphis departs the temple of Isis a new man: darker-complexioned, sharper-featured, shorter-haired, more vigorous, her powers enhanced, *vires augentur* (787–9), and so also, one may presume, though Ovid decorously refrains from specifying this key feature, newly equipped with his own virile appendage.[25] So the book that opens with a horn lost ends happily with a horn gained. And Iphis' triumph over castration contains the figurative remedy not just for Achelous and Nisus but above all for Scylla – Scylla who is, after all, a girl in want of

---

[24] Though these "horns" are the streams of the Nile delta, one wonders if this many-horned river isn't also a reply to the dehorned Achelous.

[25] See Wheeler (1997): Iphis ( = *vires*) thus finally realizes the promise of his/her name. Cf. Scylla's leap, *faciente cupidine **vires***, at 8.143; not a god but her own desire supplies Scylla with what she lacks.

a phallus, just like Iphis. The fine paradox of this conjunction is that Iphis is turned into a boy as a reward for her consistently feminine, passive, and unassuming stance, whereas Scylla, who makes an aggressive play for the phallus, is never allowed to have it.

One reason all these episodes of horns and dehorning show up at the extremes of their books is that this location aligns their storied losses and gains with the knobs projecting from either end of the rod around which the book would have been rolled. Those knobs were known as "horns," *cornua*, and the rolled edge from which each projected was the book's *frons* or brow. To read a book to the end, in one Latin idiom, is to read it *ad cornua*. In the case of *Metamorphoses* 8, we read *ad cornua* only to discover that one horn is missing – Achelous' horn, that is.[26] However maimed in reality, the bookroll always sports a virtual pair of horns. Indeed, it may be that the only character on the Ovidian scene with an indubitably full set of horns is the author himself. Certainly the horned bookroll would make an excellent frontispiece for the *Metamorphoses*, one betokening the seemingly inexhaustible fecundity of the Ovidian imagination. Another appealing candidate can be extracted from the end of *Metamorphoses* 9, where Isis visits the mother of Iphis accompanied by her retinue of exotic Egyptian gods, among them her consort Osiris: Osiris, the god who was torn to pieces, and then painstakingly pieced back together by Isis, after she had searched the world for his scattered members. When Ovid describes Osiris as "never sufficiently sought for" (*numquamque satis quaesitus Osiris*, 9.693), he may be thinking of the version of the myth in which Isis never did find all of Osiris; the restoration was incomplete. It was, of course, the god's privates that went forever missing. It was in response to this gap in the body of Osiris that Isis fashioned her mimetic replica of the missing part – the original phallus.[27] But there is less difference between the well-equipped bookroll and the patched-up Osiris than might at first appear. In the *Metamorphoses*, lack is expressed not as a tragic absence but as an enabling dislocation and comic multiplication of meanings. There are always extra horns around waiting their turn in the story.

[26] So Holzberg (1998) 84.
[27] See Diod. Sic. 1.21.5, 1.22.6; Plut. *De Is. et Osir.* 358b.

## *Relicta sine viro*: Catullus and the rhetoric of castration

In the previous section I meant to keep my sights trained on penis envy. But the topic tends inevitably, and especially in the case of a girl such as Scylla, so very far from resigned to her feminine plight, to conjure up the specter of castration anxiety. One of the most spectacular incarnations of this anxiety is the fabled Attis, the self-castrated consort of the mother-goddess Cybele, and the protagonist of Catullus 63. Castration is, indeed, the very first event of which that poem takes account, the burden (breathlessly delayed by a series of scene-setting subordinate clauses) of its first sentence (*devolsit ipse acuto sibi pondera silice*, 63.5).[28] There follows a miniature tragedy, with Attis, now provocatively "she" instead of he,[29] summoning "her" companions in an ecstatic procession to the goddess, and then, after dropping exhausted into sleep at the goddess's doorstep, waking up to recognize and lament, with belated lucidity, what "she" has done. Cybele responds by sending one of her lions to round up her errant devotee, and the poem concludes with Catullus earnestly praying her brand of madness away from himself and his household.

Though the subject matter may seem to solicit a Freudian approach, there are good reasons to resist the solicitation. Not only is Catullus' "castration anxiety" right at the surface; it has an objective correlative in contemporary experience. A Roman boy need not have resorted to misreading the body of a Roman girl to discover that castration was "for real." There were plenty of real live eunuchs to be seen in Rome, and especially on those festival days when the castrated priests of the Magna Mater poured out of their temple precinct, making their strange music, dancing their wild dances, and (a most unpriestly occupation) begging for alms.[30] Anxiety was a predictable reaction to these flamboyant creatures, who sounded and looked and acted so unRoman and were yet so intimately associated with a Roman goddess – as the Great Idaean Mother, a fixture in the city for well over a century, and equipped with

[28] Reading *ipse* for the OCT *ili*, following Currie (1996) (with thanks to Norbert Lain for the reference).

[29] A tonic reminder in Gardner (1998) 137: "Roman lawyers did not even consider the possibility of regarding *castrati* as female. Once a man, always a man."

[30] Beard (1994).

an imposing temple and an important state festival, perhaps deserves to be called.[31] True, there was a sharp distinction (knife-sharp, in fact) between the Mother's Roman patrons and her Phrygian priests. But the latter served as a reminder of what men could and did suffer in their devotion to her service.

One might propose that the ubiquity of castrati, including household slaves (castrati were luxury items in elite households) as well as the exotic *galli*, far from defusing castration anxiety, would make it the more efficacious by removing it from the realm of mere fantasy. Yet the charter myth of the *galli* does not provide the Freudian critic with much traction either. For Freud, the function of castration anxiety is to precipitate the dissolution of the Oedipus complex: with his most cherished part under threat, the little boy gives up his desire for his mother and internalizes his father. But this is hardly Attis' story. In the common version of the myth, Attis is punished for straying from the Mother and dallying with a nymph: he is punished, that is, not for clinging to but for abandoning the original maternal object of desire. True, Catullus gives us a different Attis, not the Mother's unfaithful lover, but a young man driven to frenzy by what Attis calls "excessive hatred of Venus," *Veneris nimio odio* (63.17). Instead of making the transition into normative sexuality, this Attis resists adult sexuality altogether. Were one to seek a psychoanalytic fable to which the myth might be matched (in either version), one might have recourse to the Jungian mother-archetype, or Klein's terrifying maternal fantasies, or Lacan's account of the fragmented ego on the other side of the (maternal) mirror stage, but not, it seems, to the Freudian castration complex.

Another obstacle to a Freudian approach is presented by the decidedly homoerotic ambit of the Catullan Attis, who is fashioned, it emerges, in the mold of a familiar Greek stereotype: that of the beautiful youth, glamorous object of masculine admiration. It is this celebrity status that Attis seems most to regret when he comes to his senses; it is his fond recollections of his glory days as "flower of the gymnasium" and much-courted favorite (63.64–7) that form the core of his lament. For Freud,

---

[31] Full discussion of the introduction of the cult in Roller (1999) 263–320; Wiseman (1985) 198–206 suggests that Catull. 63 was composed for performance at the Megalesia.

femininity posed a special challenge, since the little girl has to change not only the object but the orientation of her desire; the little boy, by contrast, has only to replace his mother with another woman.[32] For Catullus, the case is different. Whereas Freud saw girls as little men, Roman sexual ideology sees boys as little women: potentially penetrable objects, inviting or fending off desire, but not themselves active subjects of desire. Latin poetry is full of images of seductive boys, boys hardly distinguishable from girls, with the peach fuzz on their cheeks intensifying their attraction as it warns of their imminent passage into adulthood. As Marilyn Skinner points out, what sets Attis apart is the intensity of his resistance to crossing over: it is because he cannot face the "painful struggle for psychosexual autonomy required to effect his transformation into a fully functioning adult male" that he resorts to self-mutilation, hoping thereby to fix himself "at the passive stage."[33] The castration of Attis is a hyperliteralization of puerile lack which turns the boy into a real (fake) "little woman" for good.

The long poems are preoccupied with the theme of marriage, a theme trumpeted in the explicitly epithalamic 61 and 62 and varied in poems 64 to 68, which treat of marriages contemporary and mythological, scandalous and sublime, happily prolonged and tragically cut short. Attis has been shown to belong in this company in that he displays features of both the impetuous groom, speeding eagerly toward his divine consort, and (especially) the reluctant bride, fair-skinned and delicate and regretting the home she has left behind.[34] Yet were Attis to seek his reflection in the long poems, he might find it not in the husband or bride but in the slave *concubinus* (Attis too will end as a slave, *famula*, 63.90) who supplies poem 61 with a target for the stylized mockery that is a conventional feature of the wedding song.[35] Smooth-cheeked and long-haired, this epicene figure encapsulates the premarital sexual distractions the bridegroom is to give up. In a lyric setting the beautiful slave might be the object of praise. But within the epithalamium, with its characteristic emphasis on georgic productivity and fruitfulness, he is viewed in negative terms as *iners* (61.124), "lazy" or unproductive. Homoerotic "playtime" is officially over, both for the husband embarking on his marital career and also for the concubine,

---

[32] Freud (1925) 251.     [33] Skinner (1997) 137.     [34] E.g., Sandy (1971).
[35] Cf. Quinn (1972) 249–52.

destined perhaps, now that his boyish curls have been clipped,[36] to labor alongside the country slave-women whose advances he once scorned. The lament of Attis thus turns the epithalamium inside out, recomposing it from the perspective of a boy whose exclusion helps define the institution of marriage.

It is strange but true that Freud nowhere associates the loss of virginity with castration, or associates the two only in that the man who deflowers a virgin runs the risk of arousing her penis envy.[37] For Freud, castration anxiety is strictly a masculine complaint; what women suffer should rather be termed a disappointment. Here the Lacanian understanding of castration opens up a perspective that Freud's emphasis on bodily difference occludes. For what the marriage poems suggest is that it is not the groom but the bride who suffers symbolic castration en route to assuming her normative role; marriage both inflicts the wound and repairs it – indeed, inflicts it so as to repair it. The rhetoric of "defloration" (only a figure in Latin, not a quasi-technical term as in English, but expressive nonetheless) depicts marriage as a loss: the "flowery" bride is plucked from her "mother's lap" (61.57–9), "carried off" from the company of her peers (62.32), so that her "chaste bloom" can in turn be plucked from her (62.46).[38] Partings create parts. In the admonition with which the debate of 62 abruptly closes, the bride is instructed to yield to her husband on the grounds that her virginity is not entirely her own, *virginitas non tota tua est* (62): a third part (*tertia pars*, 63) is her father's, another part her mother's, and they have given their shares to their son-in-law (63–5). The argument is benignly quotidian, even, in its pedantic precision, disarmingly self-parodic. Yet the effect is to alienate the maid from her maidenhood. Like the castrated Attis (*ego mei pars*, 63.69), the *virgo* shorn of her *virginitas* is reduced to part of herself.[39] It is the

---

[36] *nunc tuum cinerarius | tondet os* (61.131–2) conflates the haircut with the first shave (as if the slave's beard had sprouted in instant response to the marriage).

[37] Thus Freud (1918).

[38] Defloration as castration: Putnam (1982) 22–3, connecting Attis' *flos* with the ruined bridal/virile flower at the end of Catull. 11.

[39] Appearing thrice in the rest of the corpus, *pars* is found nine times in the long poems, five instances clustered at the end of the ecphrasis of 64, where the Bacchic rout that comes for Ariadne *parte ex alia* (251) is itself in parts (*pars* four times in as many lines, 256–9); one such "part" is tossing about the body-parts, *membra*, of a calf they have torn apart.

husband who will provide compensation for her forfeited integrity, ideally in the form of a son (for example, the "darling little Torquatus" whose birth is anticipated at 61.209, a miniature duplicate of the father nestled in the mother's lap, as the bride once in her own mother's lap) – a compensatory equivalence that returns us to the castration complex, albeit one that involves defective girls, not anxious boys, and that identifies this defect as a product of culture, not nature.

I recognize that all this talk of castration (as opposed to the more neutral "loss") may seem tendentious. But there are good textual grounds for retaining the more specific term. Interpretations of the long poems generally absorb the aberrant 63 by processing Attis as a problematic "bride," mirroring the distraught Ariadne of 64. What my reading is designed to show is that it is also possible to reverse this interpretive orientation, placing Attis at the center of the long poems and processing Ariadne and her kin as figurative castrates. Such a reversal is facilitated by the uncanny description of Attis' dawning awareness, right after he has taken a "sharp flint" to his "weights" ( = testicles, 63.5), of what he has lost: "and so, when s/he became aware that her members were left manless ..." (*itaque ut relicta sensit sibi membra sine viro*, 6). My "manless" attempts to capture the strangeness of Catullus' *sine viro*, an unprecedented metonymy, reiterated a few lines later in Attis' use of the rare verb *evirare* ("you have taken the man from your bodies," *corpus evirastis*, 17).[40] If we concentrate on the literal sense of the phrase, especially in conjunction with the participle *relicta* (modifying *membra*, but also potentially describing the now-feminine subject of the sentence), another figure comes into focus alongside Attis: that of the woman literally "left without a man," where "man" can also bear its common sense of "husband." The phrase *relicta sine viro* thus operates as a subterranean passage connecting the castrated Attis with the "abandoned women" of the long poems: Ariadne in 64, Berenice in 66, Laudamia in 68.

This figurative tangle – marriage as castration and as phallic restoration, with the risk of renewed loss always on the horizon – is played out, and wittily played with, in poem 66, the translation of Callimachus'

---

[40] Catullus provides Adams's first example of this usage, followed a century later by Lucan; see Adams (1982) 70; and cf. Godwin (1995) 125 ("one would expect Attis to be a *vir* without a *membrum*, rather than *membra* without a *vir*").

"Lock of Berenice" that Catullus attached to his letter to Hortalus ( = poem 65) by way of discharging a poetic debt. Parted from her royal husband soon after their marriage, Queen Berenice vowed to sacrifice a lock of her hair upon his safe return; this poem, spoken by the severed lock from the starry eminence to which "she" was transported from the temple of Arsinoe-Aphrodite where she was originally deposited, is the outcome of that vow, commemorating both the division of lock from head and the reunion of wife with husband. The phallic value of the lock is implicit in the sacrificial economy that underpins the poem: the severed part that pays for the bridegroom's return is equivalent to the virile part for which it is exchanged. It is underwritten as well by local Alexandrian traditions which, though perhaps obscure to Catullus, have left their mark on the poem he chose to translate; as Steven Jackson has shown, Callimachus played up the kinship of his queen's lock with the so-called "lock of Isis," a precious red coral "well known for its phallic character" (a hunk was likely housed in the temple where Berenice's tress sojourned).[41] Whether or not Catullus knew about the lock of Isis, the interplay of poem 66 with poem 63, which likewise involves the severing of a body-part (albeit one that drops heavily to earth instead of soaring weightless into the sky), yields another phallic counterpart closer to home.[42]

This is perhaps to press the resemblance indelicately far, especially given that what Attis attacks is most likely not his penis but his testicles. What becomes of the much-touted phallus if castration leaves the penis intact – leaves it, in so many scandalous cases, as capable as any ordinary penis of mimicking the phallus in erection?[43] The recourse to reference, while a tonic reminder of the real practices informing the poem, here threatens to pitch us into the referential fallacy. The reign of the phallus is not ended by the recognition that castration normally leaves the penis unscathed. No doubt Freud could have chosen a term with less historical baggage (ecphallosis? depenistration?). But my point is that the lock does conjure up Attis' lost virility, even if only by way of a spectral, metonymic extension. The argument may be bolstered by the correspondence between the lost lock of Nisus and the belatedly

[41] Jackson (2001), esp. 4–5.
[42] So, e.g., Martin (1992) 175 and (cautiously) Godwin (1995) 207.
[43] The foundational complaint, in essence, of Taylor (2000).

116

acquired *vires* of Iphis, a correspondence that helps organize the central books of Ovid's *Metamorphoses*, as we have seen. Ovid seems in fact to be quite fond of this association. In his version of the Attis story in the *Fasti*, Ovid not only explicitly extends the scope of the injury – his Attis, impeccably thorough, leaves behind "no sign of the man" (*nulla ... signa relicta viri*, 4.242) – but links it, quite gratuitously, with an injury to his hair: "He even tore at his body with a sharp rock, and his long hair dragged in the squalid dust" (*ille etiam saxo corpus laniavit acuto, | longaque in immundo pulvere tracta coma est*, 237–8). The illogical sequence, which produces the vague impression that Attis has just given himself a haircut, sets the pattern for Cybele's priests, who "toss their hair about and slice their worthless members" (*caedunt iactatis vilia membra comis*, 244) – an even tighter juxtaposition of severable parts, though normalized as a scene of quasi-bacchantic revelry. It is almost as if Ovid meant to underscore the figurative identification of lock and phallus by compressing into a single scene what Catullus had distributed over two poems.[44]

If the whole man can stand for the virile part, as in the phrase *sine viro*, the part can also stand for the whole. As Virgil's notorious allusion to this passage suggests, the lock's protestations, "against my will, o queen, did I leave your head, against my will!" (*invita, o regina, tuo de vertice cessi, | invita*, 66.39–40, quoted almost verbatim at Virg. *Aen.* 6.460, where Aeneas assures Dido's shade that he abandoned her against *his* will), align her with the man whose departure she reenacts and whose faithlessness she disavows. Unlike Dido, however, Berenice, lockless but not *sine viro*, can laugh at the one "betrayal," since it has saved her from the permanent consequences of the other. Overlaid on this identification is another, equally predictable. "It was just after I had been severed," the lock recollects, "and my sister locks were mourning my fate ..." (*abiunctae paulo ante comae mea fata sorores | lugebant*, 51–2): the lock thus tragically parted from her "sister locks" reenacts the departure of the bride from the sad chorus of her peers, a separation lamented (without a trace of urbane irony) in poem 62. Catullus' use of *abiunctae* to render Callimachus' more neutral "newly cut" (νεότμητον) underscores the point: the bride's dis-joining is the necessary complement of the marital conjunction, marriage contemplated from the side of loss.

---

[44] And the story continues into Statius' *Achilleid*: see Heslin (2005) 260.

That loss can be grim indeed. The lock's complaints against the irresistible force of iron ("What are locks to do, when such great objects [as Mount Athos] yield to iron?" 47) may remind readers of another virgin fated to succumb to iron (*ferro*, 64.369), as the Fates foretell near the end of poem 64; this is Polyxena, destined to be sacrificed – in Catullus' unusually grisly version, to have her head cut off (*truncum ... corpus*, 370) – at the grave of Achilles after the fall of Troy. The "tragic marriage" of Polyxena cashes out the hyperbolic rhetoric of the girls of 62, who compare the bride's surrender to the evils meted out to a conquered city ("What does the enemy do after capturing a city that is more cruel than that?" 62.24; one thinks inevitably of Troy, a constant point of reference in the long poems). But the beheading of the virgin also communicates with its blackly humorous transformation in the "beheading" of the lock, doomed to fall to iron scissors on the altar of remarriage.

This mock-tragedy seems to purge marriage of its darker emotions, leaving earthbound brides free to leap gladly (back) into bed.[45] Accordingly, before she falls silent, the lock institutes a form of ritual compensation. Newlywed brides are henceforth to pour out a jar of perfume for the lock to enjoy (66.80–3):

> non prius unanimis corpora coniugibus
> tradite nudantes reiecta veste papillas,
> quam iucunda mihi munera libet onyx,
> vester onyx, casto colitis quae iura cubili.

wait to turn your bodies over to your likeminded husbands, throwing off your clothes and baring your nipples, until the onyx jar offers me the libation I enjoy – the onyx jar, I mean, belonging to those of you who are law-abiding and keep your bed chaste.

Like the master of ceremonies in poem 61, the lock is eager at once to encourage and to circumscribe sexual pleasure within marriage. Hence the restrictive iteration of *vester onyx*: the lock spurns offerings from the adulterous. It is natural for the lock to ask for perfume (a feature of coiffure in which Berenice took special interest), and the precious onyx

---

[45] I am leaving aside the specifically Alexandrian sexuality that Catullus is translating here; on the eroticized marriage in court propaganda, see Gutzwiller (1992).

makes an unexceptionable receptacle. Yet the corporeal sense of *onyx* (= "fingernail") may also be in play. It is as if the severed lock were demanding its own equivalent, in the shape of another severable body-part, a "nail" of celebratory perfume.[46] Once again we are reminded that symbolic castration is the price paid for the acquisition of a *vir*.

Thus far I have been taking up castration as a Catullan figure: as a way of representing what happens to a woman when she passes into and out of marriage. The unFreudian implication (unFreudian, because for Freud the woman is "castrated" to begin with) is that the woman has to be cut down to size so as to accommodate a husband: rendered partial so as to be made whole. However, one could also turn the argument around and take this representation as a projection of the man's anxiety, as if it were the man who required a feminine prosthesis tailored to his own lack. (After all, Attis is not a symbolically castrated woman but a literally castrated man.) I began my discussion of Attis by laying out some of the local obstacles to a Freudian approach, and while those obstacles remain as firmly in place as ever, I want all the same to end this discussion by experimenting with just such an approach. The experiment involves treating castration not as a figure (Berenice *sine viro* is "castrated," etc.) but as something against which the text (or Catullus?) marshals all its (his?) figurative resources. Two Catullan habits of figuration will occupy me in particular: synecdoche and what I will call vocalization.

Synecdoche I take to be the rhetorical counterpart of the fetish: the substitution of part for part. As Freud defines it, the fetish is itself a figure, "a substitute for the woman's (the mother's) penis that the little boy once believed in and – for reasons familiar to us – does not want to give up."[47] For Freud, fetishism is an alternative outcome to the oedipal drama: instead of bowing to the paternal prohibition, the fetishist simply declines to accept the evidence of castration furnished by the woman's body. Turning his eyes from the horrifying sight of what is not there, the fetishist fixes on something (anything!) that is (a bit of fur, a shoe, an article of clothing), which he thenceforth adopts as a place-holder for the mother's phallus, thereby simultaneously denying and acknowledging the reality of her lack. If we make the experiment of

[46] Cf. Jackson (2001) 7, associating the onyx with the phallic *basanites*.
[47] Freud (1927) 152–3.

looking through a fetishist's eyes at Ariadne,[48] the most famous "abandoned woman" of the long poems, as she gazes from the shore after Theseus' departing ship, what we will see is a woman's body seductively ashimmer with the alternating movements of veiling and revealing, a kind of pictorial litotes ("not covered") (64.63–7):

> non flavo retinens subtilem vertice mitram,
> non contecta levi velatum pectus amictu,
> non tereti strophio lactentis vincta papillas,
> omnia quae toto delapsa e corpore passim
> ipsius ante pedes fluctus salis alludebant.

Not keeping the fine veil on her blonde head, not covered up with chest veiled by a thin cloth, not binding with smooth breastband her milky nipples – all of which, having slipped from her whole body regardless, became the plaything of the salt waves at her feet.

Ariadne *relicta sine viro* is also Ariadne castrated, not just figuratively but corporeally, something this description avoids knowing by traveling directly from Ariadne's head and breasts to her feet, overleaping the (missing) parts in between, and thereby preserving the illusion that Ariadne's body is "whole" (cf. *toto … corpore*, 66).

One might object that the blazon is designed to meet the demands of erotic and poetic decorum; this is hardly the place for Catullus to focus on Ariadne's genitals. Yet the fetishizing argument is bolstered by one odd detail at least. The image of Ariadne's "milky nipples," *lactentis … papillas* (64.65), is readily processed as a twofold metonymy (= "white breasts"). But if we stop long enough to take in the literal meaning, we find ourselves confronted with a lactating mother. Compare the description of the sea-nymphs in the framing Argonautic narrative as they rise up to marvel at the passage of the world's first ship: "Nymphs with bodies bared, projecting as far as their 'nursers' from the white whirl" (*nudato corpore Nymphas, / nutricum tenus exstantes e gurgite cano*, 17–18). Like Ariadne, the nymphs are too distracted by what they are seeing to think about being seen. And like Ariadne, they have breasts ("nursers," a Catullan coinage after the Greek τίτθη) pregnant

---

[48] Cf. Fitzgerald (1995) 147–9, invoking castration anxiety in service of a different reading.

with maternity. As with Ariadne, again, these maternal parts replace the whole body the passage seemed to promise (*nudato corpore*, 17). We look at the maternal breasts, not (and in place of) the mother's missing phallus, which persists as a possibility beneath the veil of (milky?) white foam under which Catullus has submerged it.

The description of Ariadne ends at her feet (*ipsius ante pedes*, 64.67). The detail is unobtrusive, but it gathers significance from the over-arching marriage theme in which Ariadne is embedded. Unlike the bride whose feet pass felicitously over the threshold in poem 61 (*transfer omine cum bono / limen aureolos pedes*, 159–60), the tapestry-Ariadne is permanently arrested at the border of land and sea. Yet the foot is also, of course, the most notorious of fetishes, a phallic stand-in with a venerable pedigree. And there are, in fact, a surprising number of flashy feet on offer in the long poems.[49] Gratuitous refer-ences to feet are strewn across the Attis poem, from the "agitated foot" with which Attis first "eagerly" touches Phrygia (*citato cupide pede*, 63.2), to the "speeding foot" of Cybele's new devotees (*properante pede*, 30; *properipedem*, 34) as they rush to join her "excited three-foot dances" (*citatis celerare tripudiis*, 26), to the "roaming foot" (*pede vago*, 86) of the lion she dispatches to bring Attis back into the fold.[50] Freud might take these multiplying members, like the snakes on Medusa's head, to signify castration by way of a reiterated denial of castration.[51] One might equally well venture a self-reflexive explana-tion: the speeding feet of the *galli* embody the excited feet of the galliambic meter, a rare form associated, as its name suggests, with the priests of Cybele, and used by Catullus only here. If the iamb is a *pes citus*, as Horace describes it in the *Ars Poetica* (*Ars* 252), the galliamb, with its characteristic runs of light syllables (the norm is four or even five in a row in the second half of the line), is the ultimate *pes citatus*; I would venture to describe it as a castrated meter, custom-made for the man of unRoman *levitas*, a man whose first action is to disburden himself of his genital "weights" (*pondera*, 5). The metrical reading thus circles back around to a Freudian conclusion.

---

[49] Cf. Janan (1994) 127–30.

[50] Also *vegetis sonipedibus*, 41; *pedem*, 52; the repeated *citat-* (most often *citatis*) pseudo-etymologizes "Attis."

[51] Freud (1922).

Whereas the Attis poem presents many feet in motion, poem 68 trains the spotlight on a single, motionless foot: the "soft foot" of Catullus' "radiant goddess" (*molli candida diva pede*, 70), its "gleaming sole" arrested on a "worn threshold" that we never see it cross (*trito fulgentem in limine plantam*, 71). This foot deserves to be described as a fetish in the ordinary sense of a peculiarly fascinating object, imaginatively lingered over as it lingers there on the stoop. But it may also be viewed as a fetish in the stricter sense. The description of the foot *fulgentem in limine* ("gleaming on the threshold") recalls the lock of Berenice, *caelesti in lumine ... fulgentem*, "gleaming" in the "light" of the heavens (66.7, 9; and again, *in lumine caeli ... fulgeremus*, 59, 61): it is as if the strangely effulgent foot had inherited the phallic aura of the lock. What sets such fetishes apart from the garden-variety "phallic symbol" is their resolute, ineradicable figurality. The lock of Nisus, being in any case a talisman of virile potency, loses nothing through being identified with the phallus; the identification is just a metonymic extension of the meaning it already carries, useful chiefly insofar as it facilitates connections across the text (with the horn of Achelous, or with Scylla herself when she is cut off from Minos' ship). But the fetish only works its magic so long as it holds out against this identification. One stares at the fetish so as not to see what is missing – but nothing *is* missing; there is the fetish to prove it!

Why not forget about the phallus, then, and take the fetish as a generalized figure screening loss? The argument might then rejoin the reading of the long poems proposed in my first chapter: the "soft foot" with its "gleaming sole" is fetish-like (say) insofar as it assists Catullus in not knowing what he knows: that his figures are mere fictions, his "goddess" no goddess, their "marriage" no marriage. One last famous foot pleads for inclusion in this story, and that is the "wan foot" of Catullus' brother, lapped by Lethe at the threshold of the underworld in poem 65 (*Lethaeo gurgite fratris | pallidulum manans alluit unda pedem*, 5–6). Perched at the boundary of the underworld, the brother is dead but not, it seems, quite gone. Before the poem is over, his Lethe-washed foot will have been displaced by the hotly blushing cheeks of the forgetful girl who has let her apple spill out of her lap, another figure that repudiates loss as it recollects it.[52] The same melancholy tune plays in

[52] Full discussion above, 27–32.

Catullus' witty elegy for the pet sparrow that used to nestle, like the apple of 65, in a girl's "lap" (*gremio*, 3.8). Oddly enough, like poem 65, this elegy also ends with something red: "Wretched little sparrow! It's your doing now that my girlfriend's sweet eyes are red and swollen with crying," *flendo turgiduli rubent ocelli* (3.16–18).[53] Though the poem seems to turn against the sparrow, now blamed more than loved, the dead pet continues to travel with the lovers: the girlfriend's "red and swollen eyes" carry the impress of the creature she "used to love more than her own eyes" (*quem plus illa oculis suis amabat*, 5).

Such moments open up the possibility of demoting the phallus from its place of privilege – replacing castration with loss, and castration anxiety with mourning. This is a possibility to which I will return. And yet it must be acknowledged that the sparrow elegy does not take us very far from the phallus. To the contrary, the Catullan sparrow is one of the most notorious "phallic symbols" of ancient poetry, repeatedly identified (though almost as often rejected) as a stand-in for the speaker's own "dead" member (the poem is then sometimes transcribed as an allegory of impotence, with the mistress shedding tears of erotic frustration over the inert instrument of her former pleasures).[54] While I find this reading unconvincing (chiefly because its allegorical specificity eradicates the erotic charge of these poems while making nonsense of the envy that infects poem 2 in particular), I agree with Micaela Janan that its very tenacity is symptomatic, constituting a response, in Janan's words, "to a slipperiness in the text that cries out for explanation." In fact, as Janan shows, the *passer* makes as good a case for the Lacanian phallus (as distinguished from the personal penis) as one is likely to find. Capable as it is of assuaging the desire of both parties equally, masculine in gender but compared to a "little girl," the bird's "very lack of specificity makes it *the* object of exchange, *the* sexual signifier – a fetishized object charged with Catullus' displaced desire for Lesbia." Janan then proceeds with the classic Lacanian gesture of abstraction: "By retaining the concept of 'loss' from impotence, while discarding literal detumescence, we can see the larger concept of 'castration' adduced here – castration in the Lacanian sense, an

[53] Poems 3 and 65 are persuasively connected by Wray (2001) 200–3 on other grounds.
[54] See, e.g., with bibliography on both sides, Hooper (1985); the argument involves Catullus 2 as well, of course.

irremediable lack in the subject."[55] My one qualification, but to my mind an important one, marking the divergence of the Freudian from the Lacanian reading, is that this generalized "lack" is specified – fleshed out, as it were – by the final line, which reincorporates the phallus, along with the sparrow, in the "red and swollen" eyes of the mistress. These eyes simultaneously register castration and deny it: mourn the phallus and resurrect it. In effect, another fetish.

In my discussion of Philomela in chapter 2, I explored the chain of substitutions, phallus–tongue–child, that helps organize Ovid's fable of *libertas* begotten and aborted. This identification, it is worth reiterating, is buttressed by metonymic association (speech being marked as a masculine privilege) as well as the iconic resemblance of the twinned protuberances.[56] If the fetish sidesteps castration, vocalization may go some way toward counteracting it. The idea I would like to entertain, for the space of one paragraph at least, is that the promotion of voice in Catullus' long poems is itself a defense against castration anxiety.

Certainly the Attis poem performs a flamboyant refusal of muteness. It is not just that the poem repeatedly alludes to sound (chanting, howls, barbarous music, followed by Attis' extended lament by the shore) but that it loudly reproduces, with its insistent alliterations and semi-rhymes tumbling through wild galliambics, the strange music of Cybele's retinue. The very markedness of the form turns the reader into an unusually self-conscious performer, with a heightened sense of laboring breath, throat, and tongue, thereby reassuring him that *his* body at least is still (all) there. Moreover, though noisiness may be a predictable feature of Catullus' exotic theme, the long poems provide other, stranger examples of muteness overcome. The most famous is the ecphrasis of poem 64, a piece of speechless cloth that bears the impassioned soliloquy of its embroidered heroine as well as the uproar of the Bacchic company coming to claim her.[57] Indeed, the rhetorical

---

[55] Janan (1994) 47.

[56] Both aspects are exploited in Phaedrus' fable on the phallic origins of the female tongue; see above, 85. In poem 74 Catullus supplies his own obscenely literal illustration by associating fellatio with muteness; a mouth thus filled can't deploy its own tongue.

[57] Though the "actual" tapestry is distinguished from the narrator's digressions, including the speech of Ariadne (see above, 45–6), one is repeatedly seduced into believing that Ariadne is "really" speaking, not least because the ecphrasis is

amplifications of that soliloquy, the bravura onomatopoetics of that uproar, seem designed to pierce the enshrouding silence, as if turning up the volume could render these inaudible ecphrastic figures audible. Elsewhere it is literally tongueless things that are given voice: the stellified lock of Berenice, whose speech is coextensive with poem 66, and the chatty Veronese house-door of poem 67, believed to be tongue-less and earless by her mistress, but capable even so of spilling the secrets of her household to her inquiring interlocutor. Taken up via the thematics of the Attis poem, these prosthetic voices, the artificiality of which is ever more apparent, seem designed as replacements for the missing phallus.

At this point it would be possible, once again, to turn the discussion around, promoting mourning over castration and reading this insistent voicedness as an oblique response to Catullus' inability to bring his brother back to life. After all, Latin speakers refer to the dead as, precisely, those who no longer speak: the "silent ones" (*silentes*).[58] As Michaela Schmale has observed, when he compares his tapestry-Ariadne to a "stony statue of a Bacchant" (*saxea ut effigies bacchantis*, 64.61), Catullus sets up the subsequent Pygmalion-effect of his own ecphrastic art, which will bring the "dead" image to agitated life (every ecphrasis, Schmale notes, plays with the boundary between death and life, but none more flagrantly than this one).[59] Viewed from this angle, the description of the *Argo* at the start of poem 64 acquires a new urgency, featuring as it does an artifact famously endowed with the ability to speak (courtesy of Athena, who wove a Dodonaean plank into its fabric).[60] If Catullus suppresses this detail, it is to make room for his own vitalizing rhetoric: his *Argo* is constructed out of mountain-"born" pines that "swim" the sea carrying Argive "oak" ( = "manpower") plying "hands of fir" (*prognatae*, 1; *nasse*, 2; *robora*, 4; *abiegnis ... palmis*, 7).[61] It is because he cannot

---

saturated throughout, and from the very start (*namque fluentisono*, 64.62), with sound and motion; see Laird (1993).

[58] Feldherr (2000) 216.    [59] Schmale (2004) 153–5, 170–3.

[60] Ap. Rh. *Arg.* 1.524–7, 4.580–3; I owe this suggestion to Darcy Krasne.

[61] For these and other observations, see the richly detailed discussion of poem 64 in Young (2008).

reanimate the brother buried at Troy that he keeps on animating what dead things he can: a ship, a tapestry, a lock of hair, a door.[62]

In chapter 1, I noted that Catullus' famous elegy for his brother conducts its own quarrel with silence: muffled by the "mute ash" which renders his address vain (*et mutam nequiquam alloquerer cinerem*, 101.4), the poet's voice sings out all the louder (*heu miser indigne frater adempte mihi*, 6).[63] The living brother at least will not keep silent. The "I can't keep quiet" with which he breaks out in thanks to Allius (*non possum reticere*, 68.41) likewise frames the ensuing performance as an escape from the grave, not just for Allius but for the poet who has undertaken to rescue his name. Of course, the truth veiled by these performances is that Catullus is himself a dead poet "speaking" to us living readers from the other side of the page. In that sense, all of his poems are prosopopoetic: inanimate objects magically communicating the vivid voice entrusted to their mute surfaces. As the fetish at once embodies and forestalls the knowledge of castration, Catullus' poems both double for and mourn the voice from which they are forever cut off.

---

[62] Promoting mourning does not mean forgetting castration, of course. For psychoanalysis, these topics are intimately linked, with Lacan accenting the second term and Freud the first; see Ricciardi (2003) 17–63, with a forceful critique of Lacan's reduction of historical loss to systematic lack.

[63] Above, 16–17.

# Afterword: Freud's Rome

When Freud's *The Interpretation of Dreams* first appeared, it bore the symbolically potent publication date of 1900: the new century and the new science were to be born together.[1] The midwife attending that twin birth was none other than Virgil, who supplied Freud with his menacing epigraph: "if I cannot bend the gods above, I will rouse the underworld" (*flectere si nequeo superos, Acheronta movebo, Aen.* 7.312). A few pages from the end of the book Freud would invoke the same line "to picture the efforts of the repressed instinctual impulses" (as Freud subsequently noted); *The Interpretation of Dreams* is thus effectively bracketed by Virgil.[2] The Virgilian citation is part of the much larger story of Freud's engagement with Rome, a story that has been well told by others and that I cannot rehearse in full here.[3] My goal is to draw attention to some of its recurring themes, and especially those that bear on the

---

[1] "Psycho-analysis may be said to have been born with the twentieth century; for the publication in which it emerged before the world as something new – my *Interpretation of Dreams* – bears the date '1900'" (Freud (1923b) 191); the book actually appeared in November 1899. As Denis Feeney points out to me, the new century did not actually start until 1901, a troubling detail of which Freud evidently succeeded in remaining unaware.

[2] Freud (1900) 608; as observed by Starobinski (1987) 274–5, the framing is enhanced by the 1909 addition, immediately after the Virgilian citation, of a famous sentence that incorporates the book's title (as well as more Latin: *"The interpretation of dreams is the Via regia ..."*), thus completing the chiasmus (title/Virgil/Virgil/title).

[3] See Bellamy (1992) 38–81 (including a suggestive reading of repression in the *Aeneid*); Damrosch (1986). On the multivalence of the epigraph, Starobinski (1987), with further bibliography.

interpretive project of this book. Following Freud's lead, which happily accords with my own inclination, I begin and end with Virgil.

Let me start by noting that the choice of epigraph is surprising, and not only because Freud elected the relatively unglamorous Virgil to this important post, over the heads of the sublime Sophocles and Shakespeare and Goethe. True, the *Aeneid* was the most continuously canonical of classical texts, and a cornerstone of European education right through the nineteenth century. But if Freud wanted to sanctify his great project by associating it with Virgil's *auctoritas*, one might have expected him to identify with Aeneas, who descends into the underworld and returns safe (through the gate of dreams, no less!) with a new burden of knowledge. For Freud, the scene also has a biographical resonance: it is to meet the ghost of his dead father that Aeneas descends, a ghost Freud would likewise have to confront when he ventured into the depths of his unconscious, shortly after the death of his own father, in the course of his path-breaking self-analysis.[4] And the hero who leads his band of Trojan survivors to the promised land in Italy, setting in train the founding of a city he will not live to enter (the parallel with Freud's beloved Moses is overwhelmingly obvious), could also have supplied the founder of psychoanalysis with an image, at once grandiose and gloomy, of his own destiny.[5]

For all that, Freud chose an epigraph that aligns him not with *pius Aeneas* but with savage Juno, a goddess who is literally hell-bent on thwarting the ascendancy of Rome. But this choice too is overdetermined. As an innovator confronting a largely unappreciative Viennese establishment, Freud must have enjoyed the violent license the Junonian role afforded: the upstart scientist is effectively promising to "give 'em hell" (or to "make hell hot for them," in the German idiom).[6] And to a Jew making his way in a more or less strenuously anti-Semitic society, it cannot have been a matter of indifference that Juno was the goddess of Dido and of Hannibal; Hannibal, the brilliant Semite who boldly challenged the

---

[4] Cf. Anzieu (1986) 177. Again like Aeneas, Freud was blessed or cursed with a young and beautiful mother, whom he recollected having seen once in the nude, a memory he reported to his friend Fliess under the decorous veil of Latin; see Freud to Fliess, October 3, 1897, in Masson (1985) 268.

[5] So Damrosch (1986) 120–1: "the book's epigraph recalls Aeneas, and indeed the book seems written in the spirit of the *Aeneid*," with Freud as Aeneas (and Moses).

[6] Similarly Willbern (1979) (Freud threatening to "raise hell").

Roman (Catholic) status quo, was one of Freud's boyhood idols (indeed, Freud's analysis of his "Rome" dreams in *The Interpretation of Dreams* hinges on his identification with the Carthaginian general).[7] If Freud chose Juno over Aeneas, it was in part because to Jewish eyes the city and empire Aeneas founded would always be shrouded in ambivalence.

But though the epigraph speaks eloquently for Freud, it also speaks, and eloquently too, for his new science. Psychoanalysis really is less of an Aeneas than a Juno, impious and oppositional and allied with the forces of darkness.[8] The psychoanalyst descends into the underworld not just to find but to produce the truth; reaching down from above, as it were, he gives a hand to the repressed thoughts and desires struggling up from below. I am sure Freud knew perfectly well what he was about when he resolved to join his voice to Juno's as he stepped across the threshold of his book; I am sure he knew his epigraph was tendentious, pleasurably freighted as it is with Semitic defiance. Yet what makes the epigraph seem so inevitable, so "right," is that this extra freight does not interfere with its official function as a quasi-frontispiece or implicit illustration. To the contrary, the epigraph both provides an emblem of the irregular forces psychoanalysis will programmatically deploy and effectively launches the attack.

Whatever infernal stratagems it may illustrate, Freud's use of the Virgilian line as an illustration raises problems of its own. In the event, for the psychoanalytically inclined classicist, Freud's appropriation of classical antiquity, though sometimes invoked as an answer to the charge of anachronism, does not so much remove as itself present a theoretical stumbling-block. With its procession of monsters and monster-slaying heroes, oedipal sons and cannibalistic fathers, classical mythology was (and remains) a rich resource for those seeking vivid enactments of the

---

[7] Freud (1900) 193–8; "To my youthful mind Hannibal and Rome symbolized the conflict between the tenacity of Jewry and the organization of the Catholic church" (196). The hexameter in which Dido calls upon "someone" (Hannibal) to arise as an avenger (*Aen.* 4.625) occasions a memory-lapse analyzed at Freud (1901) 6–14, a discussion in which Catholic saints (and anti-Semitism) loom large; once again, Dido and Hannibal appear to be bound up with Jewish anxiety in the face of Catholic persecution.

[8] Again, Damrosch (1986) 113: "The destabilizing ... of the imperial conscious self is a project at the heart of Freud's ethics."

recurrent conflicts of psychic life.[9] What made the ancient material so exciting, for Freud, was the transparency with which it represented everything that a later, more civilized age would be obliged to veil. A case in point is the modern obfuscation of the once-ubiquitous phallus (Freud had occasion to admire several specimens – in a museum, naturally – on a trip to Italy in 1898): what used to be shown can be shown no longer. In Sophocles' *Oedipus* likewise, Freud remarks, the underlying childhood fantasy "is brought into the open and realized as it would be in a dream," whereas by the time of Shakespeare's *Hamlet* the curtain has fallen, and the oedipal content "remains repressed; and – just as in the case of a neurosis – we only learn of its existence from its inhibiting consequences." It is "the secular advance of repression in the emotional life of mankind" that locks away the phallus and that transforms the Sophoclean drama into a Shakespearean enigma, one no less effective for having remained so long unresolved.[10] My point is that if antiquity is the time before repression (the unabashed "infancy" of western civilization), it would seem to be located beyond interpretation. Dreams may be pervaded by "phallic symbols," but the phallus itself is not a symbol.[11] *Oedipus* enables Freud to read *Hamlet*, but Freud does not read *Oedipus*, he simply adopts the Sophoclean hero by assigning his name and history to Everyman.[12]

I have overstated the case, I know. My discussion of Ovid's Scylla in chapter 3 was meant to show that a lateral reading can be abetted by "phallic symbols" of the most obvious kind; depth is not the only interpretive criterion. Moreover, though Freud never proposed an interpretation of *Oedipus*, it was certainly more to him than the repository of his favorite myth. He was especially taken by the way the drama gradually advanced, "with cunning delays and ever-mounting excitement," toward its horrific revelation – "a process that can be likened," he noted

---

[9] Important psychoanalytic studies of Greek myths in Slater ([1968] 1992); Caldwell (1989).

[10] Freud (1900) 264; a compelling alternative account of *Hamlet* in Adelman (1992) 11–37.

[11] Freud's identification of Priapus as "a wish fulfillment representing the opposite of psychological impotence" shows how intractable he found the thing itself; Freud to Fliess, April 14, 1898, in Masson (1985) 308.

[12] E.g., "Like Oedipus, we live in ignorance of these wishes, repugnant to morality, which have been forced upon us by nature" (Freud [1900] 263).

with approval, "to the work of a psychoanalysis."[13] And the likeness does not end there. Though Freud does not mention this, the revelation is produced not just by Oedipus' detective work but, over and over again, by the wildly proliferating dramatic ironies that are so striking a feature of this play.[14] How could the author of *The Psychopathology of Everyday Life* have failed to respond to this dimension of a tragedy we know he had read and studied in Greek? Indeed, nowhere in classical literature will one find language turning more insistently and aggressively against the speaker who supposes himself to be the master of his words; Sophocles has given us an Oedipus who seems to be driven by some fearful force (the gods? the unconscious?) to keep repeating the truth of which he is unaware. For all Freud's insistence on the clarity of the ancient representation, then, one may surmise that his promotion of Oedipus had as much to do with the symptomatic texture of the Sophoclean play as with its fantastic content. Freud's writings are written by his reading of Sophocles in ways Freud cannot completely take into account; his texts have their unconscious too.

The never-banished question of anachronism has elicited an important set of responses from psychoanalytically oriented classicists. Micaela Janan began her 1994 book on Catullus, a study that did much to advance the cause of psychoanalysis in Latin literary studies, by tracing the history of the desiring subject "From Plato to Freud to Lacan" (the title of her first chapter), showing psychoanalysis to be no interloper, but a native plant with deep, ancient roots. More recently, James Porter and Mark Buchan have turned the question on its head, proposing that Lacanian theory can free us from our highly prized "fantasy of the unified subject" and enable us to see, with newly cleared vision, the fragmented, evacuated, Lacanian subjectivity that Homer and Virgil actually represent.[15] The strongest line is the one put forward by Richard Armstrong in his study of the role played by the "ancient archive" in the emergence of psychoanalysis. For Armstrong, a "meaningful dialogue"

---

[13] Freud (1900) 262.    [14] See Segal (1994a).

[15] Janan (1994) 1–36; Porter and Buchan (2004a) 11; Buchan (2004) (on Homer); Porter (2004) (on Virgil); see also Heslin (2005) 277–300 (esp. 284–6) for Statius as a forerunner of Lacan; Toohey (2004) 261–82 for a thought-provoking dialogue between Lacanian and Roman "mirror stages." Addressing anachronism head-on: Kennedy (2004).

between psychoanalysis and antiquity would involve relocating psychoanalysis within the horizon of antiquity: "the question is not whether psychoanalysis truly is the master discourse with which to unlock the real meaning of antiquity; it is rather how psychoanalysis still participates in the uncanny after-work generated by the archive of ancient culture."[16] This would mean exploring not just what Freud thought he learned or could take over from Latin literature, but what he internalized and perhaps unwittingly reproduced: psychoanalysis as a transferential effect of Freud's encounter with antiquity. In my few remaining pages, I want to toy with such an experiment, a Freudian reading of Freud's reading of Virgil, before circling back to ask what if anything such an experiment can do for my reading of Virgil.

My subject is the interaction between the *Aeneid* and *Civilization and its Discontents*. The conjunction of these two texts may be partly justified at the outset by their shared preoccupation with the costs of civilization. The *Aeneid* famously depicts the gradual evacuation of its titular hero, who is emptied of his individual desires, even of individuality as such, so as to become the vehicle and figurehead of a national destiny.[17] Having shed first Creusa and then Dido and finally Pallas too, Aeneas might, after all, have fallen in love with the fair Lavinia, his destined Italian bride. If Virgil will not so much as bring Aeneas face to face with the princess, the reason is, it seems, that only a marriage thus rigorously stripped of erotic possibility could beget the Roman empire. Freud's essay tells a similar story, one in which "civilization is built up upon a renunciation of instinct" that makes libidinal energy available for essential "civilized" sublimations (intellectual inquiry, artistic production, the ties of friendship, etc.).[18] The banality of the argument, something Freud kept acknowledging ("In none of my previous writings have I had so strong a feeling as now that what I am describing is common knowledge"),[19] may also be detected in the reading of the *Aeneid* proposed above, which doesn't mean that such a reading plays the epic

---

[16] Armstrong (2005) 5, the starting-point of a wide-ranging account of Freud's "compulsion for antiquity" (archaeology, mythology, antiquities, etc.); since Armstrong's focus is on what Freud makes of antiquity, not (so to put it) what antiquity makes of Freud, the question cited here marks one of the frontiers of his project.

[17] An excellent account in Quint (1993) 83–96.

[18] Freud (1930) 97; on the resulting (unworkable) circumscription of sexuality, 104–5.

[19] Freud (1930) 117.

false, of course. Yet taking up the epic via the polarity of pleasure and duty or individual and community seems somehow both necessary and inadequate.

Eros is one theme of both works; Thanatos is another. In Freud's argument, civilization restricts Eros in the life of the individual so as to produce ever larger human communities bound by love, all the while contending with Thanatos in the form of "the inclination to aggression," "an original, self-subsisting instinctual disposition in man," which Freud identifies as "the greatest impediment to civilization"; the latter pages of *Civilization* describe how civilization attempts to dispose of this obstacle (most notably, by sending it back inside individuals, where it "is ready to put into action against the ego the same harsh aggressiveness that the ego would have liked to satisfy upon other, extraneous individuals").[20] Any reader of the *Aeneid*, or for that matter any student of history, may wonder how Freud can identify the "combin[ing of] single human individuals, and after that families, then races, peoples and nations, into one great unity, the unity of mankind" as the work of Eros alone.[21] Eros may indeed produce empathy, a sense of belonging to the human family, but the political forms of this enlarged community tend to be accomplished by means of massive expenditures of aggression. What is missing here is the idea of imperial expansion: *imperium sine fine*, as Jupiter terms it in his promise to Venus at *Aeneid* 1.279.

This idea has not been entirely excised, however.[22] *Civilization and its Discontents* opens at something of a tangent to its topic, with Freud's reflections on the "oceanic feeling" that a friend reproached Freud for leaving out of his study of religion.[23] Freud is initially baffled by this feeling, "a sensation of 'eternity'" in which he confesses he has no share. His first attempt to grapple with it takes him into literature: "If I have

---

[20] Freud (1930) 122, 123.    [21] Freud (1930) 122.

[22] I don't mean, of course, that Freud is unaware that men are wont to go to war – see, e.g., Freud (1930) 111–15 – but that he opposes this impulse altogether to the civilizing work of Eros.

[23] In fact, it opens at a remove even from this topic, with quasi-satirical observations that are likely to strike a Latinist as quite Horatian ("It is impossible to escape the impression that people commonly use false standards of measurement – that they seek power, success and wealth for themselves and admire them in others, and that they underestimate what is of true value in life," 64), though the sentiments expressed are perfectly commonplace.

understood my friend rightly, he means the same thing by it as the consolation offered by an original and somewhat eccentric dramatist to his hero who is facing a self-inflicted death. 'We cannot fall out of this world.'"[24] The words are Hannibal's last before he kills himself in Christian Grabbe's play, and though they do not seem strikingly apt here, they do set the stage for the essay's arrival, a few pages later, where Hannibal never did, in Rome. The ostensible function of this Roman sojourn is to illustrate the persistence of the oceanic feeling, which Freud associates with the all-inclusive, undifferentiated, infantile ego, alongside the narrower "ego-feeling of maturity."[25] Freud begins by sketching the history of Rome and describing what the educated visitor to Rome can still discern of the successive stages of this history, all this as a preamble to inviting us to take a "flight of imagination": "let us ... suppose that Rome is not a human habitation but a psychical entity with a similarly long and copious past." The result is an archaeologist's dream (or nightmare) of total preservation, a Rome "in which nothing that has once come into existence will have passed away and all the earlier phases of development continue to exist alongside the latest one." In a dizzying transformation of Aeneas' visit to the site of Rome, our latter-day Evander presents us with a Rome that contains all times at once, for example: "In the place occupied by the Palazzo Caffarelli would once more stand – without the Palazzo having to be removed – the Temple of Jupiter Capitolinus; and this not only in its latest shape, as the Romans of the Empire saw it, but also in its earliest one, when it still showed Etruscan forms and was ornamented with terra-cotta antefixes."[26] The strangest thing about this amazing palimpsest is that Freud immediately proceeds to drain off its significance, first by conceding that its main value is negative (showing "how far we are from mastering the characteristics of mental life by representing them in pictorial terms") and then by admitting that a city, being subject to demolitions and disasters, is "*a priori* unsuited for a comparison of this sort."[27] One has to wonder in that case why he has included it.

---

[24] Freud (1930) 64, 65.    [25] Freud (1930) 68.

[26] Freud (1930) 70, a much-discussed passage, deployed most recently and powerfully by Gowing (2005) 155–8.

[27] Freud (1930) 71.

If the "history of the Eternal City" ("die Entwicklung der Ewige Stadt") fails as an illustration of the mind, it may yet help bring into focus the mature form of the infantile "sensation of 'eternity'" ("die Empfindung der 'Ewigkeit'").[28] Rome may be a prime specimen of a complex civilization, but it also and simultaneously embodies the imperious desire to reabsorb the world the infant had perforce to let go.[29] In a compelling reading of *Civilization and its Discontents*, Leo Bersani has drawn attention to the strange dynamic governing the relation between Freud's main text and his footnotes, the latter unfolding a very different story, one founded not on antitheses but on the threefold equation "[s]exuality = aggressiveness = civilization." For Bersani, what the literally sub-textual unconscious of *Civilization* reveals, finally, is that Freud's "civilization … is merely a cultural metaphor for the psychic fulfillment in each of us of a narcissistically thrilling wish to destroy the world."[30] My reading arrives by a different route at a similar conclusion: the oceanic feeling resurfaces as the sensation of Roman imperialism.

The undercurrent in Freud's footnotes seeps out into the text of the *Aeneid*. In the final book of the epic, Virgil's Jupiter comes to look less and less like the antithesis of Juno, and more and more like her mirror image, her sibling, even her twin.[31] The likeness culminates in Jupiter's deployment of a Dira, close kin to Juno's Allecto,[32] to chase Juturna from her brother Turnus' side, enabling Aeneas finally to bury his foundational sword in his Italian antagonist. No doubt, as Freud noted, and as Aeschylus' *Oresteia* showed, civilization requires aggression and finds uses for it. Still, something more than instrumentality is registered in Virgil's description of this event. Unlike Juno, Jupiter does not evoke his furious minister from the underworld. To the contrary, a pair of obedient Dirae are posted close at hand, "by Jove's throne, and at the threshold of the savage king" (*hae Iovis ad solium saevique in limine regis*, 12.849). While the presence of these monstrous twins in Olympus is startling, the twinned description of their master, both

---

[28] Freud ([1930] 1994) 36, 31.

[29] This is the flip (infantile) side of the image of Rome as Magna Mater discussed at the end of chapter 2; see above, 89–91.

[30] Bersani (1986) 21, 23.      [31] Excellent discussion in Hershkowitz (1998) 112–24.

[32] Or Allecto herself: so Lyne (1989) 192–4 (hence Lyne does not hesitate to render the subsequent hendiadys at 849 with a single phrase, "the savage king Jupiter," 193).

"Jove" and "savage king," is nothing less than astonishing.[33] From the poem's opening lines, which give us an Aeneas harassed by the anger of "savage Juno" (*saevae memorem Iunonis ob iram*, 1.4), the adjective *saevus* has been an index of those raging Junonian passions that it is Jupiter's task to quell or at least to contain, in a transparent allegory, in equal parts Virgilian and Freudian, of civilization keeping aggression in check. What can it mean that it is Jupiter who now qualifies as *saevus*?

Does the hendiadys encode divergent perspectives (Aeneas', Juturna's) on the supreme god (a narratological solution)? Or does the second expression expose the dark truth covered over by the august proper name thrust forward in the first? Different readers will embrace different solutions. What I want to insist on is the irreducible doubleness of the Virgilian formulation, its uncanny suspension of irreconcilable terms, sundered by the caesura, insistently reconnected by the "and" that also just prevents them from merging. The ambivalence is exacerbated by the word order, *Iovis ad solium saevique in limine regis*, where the dead-central *saevi* leans toward *Iovis* before being reined into place by the enclitic *-que*. We are left to trace and retrace the chiasmus of Jove, throne, threshold, king, with the pivotal, explosive "savage" nestled at their center. This is not a civilized critique of a civilization that has devolved into barbarity, but a redescription of civilization as aggression, at once overt and disavowed. Thus Virgil's version of *Civilization and its Discontents* sets squarely before our eyes, in plain sight though constantly sliding out of focus, the imperial problematic that Freud could not bring himself quite to write out of his *Aeneid*.

---

[33] The identification is not unanticipated; see especially *Aen.* 11.901, *ille* [sc. Turnus] *furens (et saeva Iovis sic numina poscunt)*. But to me at least the minimal space opened by the displacement of the adjective from name to *numina* makes a very big difference.

# Bibliography

(Note: *SE* = *The Standard Edition of the Complete Psychological Works of Sigmund Freud*, ed. and trans. J. Strachey et al., London, 1953–74)

Abraham, N. and Torok, M. ([1972] 1994) "Mourning or melancholia: introjection versus incorporation," in N. T. Rand (ed. and trans.) *The Shell and the Kernel*, vol. I. Chicago, 125–38

Adams, J. N. (1982) *The Latin Sexual Vocabulary*. Baltimore

Adelman, J. (1992) *Suffocating Mothers: Fantasies of Maternal Origin in Shakespeare's Plays*. New York

 (forthcoming) "Shakespeare's Romulus and Remus: who does the wolf love?," in M. del Sapio (ed.) *Identity, Otherness and Empire in Shakespeare's Rome*. Aldershot

Anderson, W. S. (1972) *Ovid's* Metamorphoses*: Books 6–10*. Norman

Armstrong, R. A. (2005) *A Compulsion for Antiquity: Freud and the Ancient World*. Ithaca

Anzieu, D. (1986) *Freud's Self-Analysis*, trans. P. Graham. Madison

Baker, S. (1960) "Lesbia's foot," *CP* 55: 171–3

Barchiesi, A. (2001) *Speaking Volumes: Narrative and Intertext in Ovid and Other Latin Poets*. London

 (2002) "Narrative technique and narratology in the *Metamorphoses*," in P. Hardie (ed.) *The Cambridge Companion to Ovid*. Cambridge, 180–99

Beard, M. (1994) "The Roman and the foreign: the cult of the 'Great Mother' in imperial Rome," in N. Thomas and C. Humphrey (eds.) *Shamanism, History, and the State*. Ann Arbor, 164–90

Bellamy, E. J. (1992) *Translations of Power: Narcissism and the Unconscious in Epic History*. Ithaca

Benjamin, J. (1995) "The omnipotent mother," in *Like Subjects, Love Objects*. New Haven, 81–113

Bersani, L. (1986) *The Freudian Body*. New York

Bettini, M. (1991) *Anthropology and Roman Culture*, trans. J. van Sickle. Baltimore

 (1999) *The Portrait of the Lover*, trans. L. Gibbs. Berkeley

Bradley, K. R. (1991) *Discovering the Roman Family*. Oxford

Brown, P. and Levinson, S. C. (1987) *Politeness: Some Universals in Language Usage*. Cambridge

Brown, S. A. (2005) *Ovid: Myth and Metamorphosis*. London

Buchan, M. (2004) "Looking to the feet: the riddles of the Scylla," in Porter and Buchan (2004b), 21–49

Burke, K. ([1939] 1973) "Freud – and the analysis of poetry," in *The Philosophy of Literary Form*. Berkeley, 258–92

Butler, J. (1993) *Bodies That Matter: On the Discursive Limits of "Sex."* New York

Butrica, J. L. (2007) "History and transmission of the text," in Skinner (2007b), 13–34

Cahoon, L. (2005) "Haunted husbands: Orpheus's song (Ovid, *Metamorphoses* 10–11) in light of Ted Hughes's *Birthday Letters*," in W. W. Batstone and G. Tissol (eds.) *Defining Genre and Gender in Latin Literature*. New York, 239–68

Caldwell, R. S. (1989) *The Origin of the Gods: A Psychoanalytic Study of Greek Theogonic Myth*. New York

Chasseguet-Smirgel, J. (1970) "Feminine guilt and the Oedipus complex," in J. Chasseguet-Smirgel (ed.) *Female Sexuality*. London, 94–134

Clauss, J. J. (1995) "A delicate foot on the well-worn threshold: paradoxical imagery in Catullus 68b," *AJP* 116: 237–53

Coleman, R. (1977) *Vergil: Eclogues*. Cambridge

Crabbe, A. (1981) "Structure and content in Ovid's *Metamorphoses*," *ANRW* II.31.4: 2274–327

Culler, J. (1984) "Textual self-consciousness and the literary unconscious," *Style* 18: 369–76

Currie, B. (1996) "A note on Catullus 63.5," *CQ* 46: 579–81

Damrosch, D. (1986) "The politics of ethics: Freud and Rome," in J. H. Smith and W. Kerrigan (eds.) *Pragmatism's Freud*. Baltimore, 102–25

Derrida, J. (1987) *The Post Card*, trans. A. Bass. Chicago

Dixon, S. (1988) *The Roman Mother*. Norman

duBois, P. (1988) *Sowing the Body: Psychoanalysis and Ancient Representations of Women*. Chicago

Elder, J. P. (1951) "Notes on some conscious and subconscious elements in Catullus' poetry," *HSCP* 60: 101–36

Enterline, L. (2000) *The Rhetoric of the Body from Ovid to Shakespeare*. Cambridge

Farrell, J. (1999) "*Aeneid* 5: poetry and parenthood," in C. Perkell (ed.) *Reading Vergil's Aeneid*. Norman, 96–110

(2005) "Intention and intertext," *Phoenix* 59: 98–111

Feeney, D. C. (1992) "'Shall I compare thee … ?' Catullus 68b and the limits of analogy," in T. Woodman and J. Powell (eds.) *Author and Audience in Latin Literature*. Cambridge, 33–44

(1995) "Criticism ancient and modern," in D. Innes, H. Hine, and C. Pelling (eds.) *Ethics and Rhetoric: Classical Essays for Donald Russell on his Seventy-Fifth Birthday*. Oxford, 301–12

Feldherr, A. (1997) "Livy's revolution: civic identity and the creation of the *res publica*," in T. Habinek and A. Schiesaro (eds.) *The Roman Cultural Revolution*. Cambridge, 136–57

(2000) "*Non inter nota sepulcra*: Catullus 101 and Roman funerary ritual," *CA* 19: 209–31

Feldman, A. B. (1962) "*Lapsus linguae* in Latin comedy," *CJ* 57: 354–5

Fitzgerald, W. (1995) *Catullan Provocations*. Berkeley

Forsyth, P. Y. (1980) "Catullus 64: Dionysus reconsidered," in C. Deroux (ed.) *Studies in Latin Literature and Roman History*, vol. II. Brussels, 98–105

Fredrick, D. (ed.) (2002) *The Roman Gaze: Vision, Power, and the Body*. Baltimore

Freud, S. (1900) *The Interpretation of Dreams*, *SE* IV; V: 339–625

(1901) *The Psychopathology of Everyday Life*, *SE* VI

(1905) *Three Essays on the Theory of Sexuality*, *SE* VII: 130–243

(1917) "Mourning and melancholia," *SE* XIV: 243–58

(1918) "The taboo of virginity," *SE* XI: 193–208

(1920) *Beyond the Pleasure Principle*, *SE* XVIII: 7–64

(1922) "Medusa's head," *SE* XVIII: 273–4

(1923a) *The Ego and the Id*, *SE* XIX: 12–66

(1923b) "A short account of psycho-analysis," *SE* XIX: 191–209

(1924) "The dissolution of the Oedipus complex," *SE* XIX: 173–9

(1925) "Some psychical consequences of the anatomical distinction between the sexes," *SE* XIX: 248–58

(1927) "Fetishism," *SE* XXI: 152–8

(1930) *Civilization and its Discontents*, SE XXI: 64–145

([1930] 1994) *Das Unbehagen in der Kultur und andere kulturtheoretische Schriften*. Frankfurt am Main

(1931) "Female sexuality," *SE* XXI: 225–43

Gaisser, J. H. (1995) "Threads in the labyrinth: competing views and voices in Catullus 64," *AJP* 116: 579–616

Galvagno, R. (1995) *Le sacrifice du corps: frayages du fantasme dans les Métamorphoses d'Ovide*. Panormitis

Gardner, J. F. (1998) "Sexing a Roman: imperfect men in Roman law," in L. Foxhall and J. Salmon (eds.) *When Men Were Men: Masculinity, Power and Identity in Classical Antiquity*. London, 136–52

Gibson, R. K. (2003) *Ovid: Ars Amatoria Book 3*. Cambridge

Gilman, S. L. (1995) *Freud, Race, and Gender*. Princeton

Godwin, J. (1995) *Catullus: Poems 61–68*. Oxford

Gowers, E. (2002) "Blind eyes and cut throats: amnesia and silence in Horace *Satires* 1.7," *CP* 97: 145–61

Gowing, A. (2005) *Empire and Memory: The Representation of the Roman Republic in Imperial Culture*. Cambridge

Griffith, M. (2005) "The subject of tragedy in Sophocles' *Antigone*," in V. Pedrick and S. Oberhelman (eds.) *The Soul of Tragedy: Essays on Athenian Drama*. Chicago, 91–135

Gunderson, E. (2003) *Declamation, Paternity, and Roman Identity*. Cambridge

Gutzwiller, K. (1992) "Callimachus' *Lock of Berenice*: fantasy, romance, and propaganda," *AJP* 113: 359–85

Hallett, C. H. (2005) *The Roman Nude: Heroic Portrait Statuary 200 BC–AD 300*. Oxford

Hardie, P. (1993) *The Epic Successors of Virgil*. Cambridge

(1994) *Virgil: Aeneid Book IX*. Cambridge

(2002) *Ovid's Poetics of Illusion*. Cambridge

(2004) "Approximative similes: incest and doubling," *Dictynna* 1: 83–112

(2006) "Virgil's Ptolemaic relations," *JRS* 96: 25–41

Hershkowitz, D. (1998) *The Madness of Epic: Reading Insanity from Homer to Statius*. Oxford

Heslin, P. J. (2005) *The Transvestite Achilles: Gender and Genre in Statius' Achilleid*. Cambridge

Hinds, S. (1998) *Allusion and Intertext*. Cambridge

Holzberg, N. (1998) "*Ter quinque volumina* as *carmen perpetuum*: the division into books in Ovid's *Metamorphoses*," *MD* 40: 77–98

(2002) *Catull: Der Dichter und sein erotisches Werk*. Munich

Hooper, R. W. (1985) "In defense of Catullus's dirty sparrow," *G&R* 32: 162–78

Horney, K. ([1926] 1967) "The flight from womanhood," in H. Kelman (ed.) *Feminine Psychology*. New York, 54–70

Hubbard, T. K. (1984) "Catullus 68: the text as self-demystification," *Arethusa* 17: 29–49

Hunter, R. (2006) *The Shadow of Callimachus: Studies in the Reception of Hellenistic Poetry at Rome*. Cambridge

Hutchinson, G. O. (2003) "The Catullan corpus, Greek epigram, and the poetry of objects," *CQ* 53: 206–21

Irigaray, L. (1991) "The bodily encounter with the mother," in M. Whitford (ed.) *The Irigaray Reader*, trans. D. Macey. Oxford, 34–46

Jackson, S. (2001) "Callimachus: *Coma Berenices*: origins," *Mnemosyne* 54: 1–9

Jacobsen, G. A. (1984) "Apollo and Tereus: parallel motifs in Ovid's *Metamorphoses*," *CJ* 80: 45–52

Janan, M. (1988) "The book of good love? Design versus desire in *Met.* 10," *Ramus* 17: 110–37

(1994) *"When the Lamp is Shattered": Desire and Narrative in Catullus*. Carbondale

(2001) *The Politics of Desire: Propertius IV*. Berkeley

Jones, E. (1927) "The early development of female sexuality," *International Journal of Psycho-Analysis* 8: 459–72

Kellum, B. (1996) "The phallus as signifier: the forum of Augustus and rituals of masculinity," in N. Kampen (ed.) *Sexuality in Ancient Art*. Cambridge, 170–83

Kennedy, D. F. (2004), "Afterword," in Porter and Buchan (2004b), 247–57

Klein, M. ([1929] 1975) "Infantile anxiety-situations reflected in a work of art and in the creative impulse," in *Love, Guilt and Reparation & Other Works 1921–1945*. London, 210–18

([1957] 1975) "Envy and gratitude," in *Envy and Gratitude & Other Works*. London, 176–235

([1963] 1975) "Some reflections on the *Oresteia*," in *Envy and Gratitude & Other Works*. London, 275–99

Knox, P. E. (1990) "Scylla's nurse," *Mnemosyne* 43: 158–9

Lacan, J. ([1953] 2006) "The function and field of speech and language in psycho-analysis," in Lacan (2006), 197–228

([1957] 2006) "The instance of the letter in the unconscious," in Lacan (2006),
412–41

([1958] 2006), "The signification of the phallus," in Lacan (2006), 575–84

([1959] 1982) "Desire and the interpretation of desire in *Hamlet*," in S. Felman (ed.)
*Literature and Psychoanalysis. The Question of Reading: Otherwise.* Baltimore,
11–52

([1964] 1981) "The Freudian unconscious and ours," in *The Four Fundamental
Concepts of Psycho-analysis*, trans. A. Sheridan. New York, 17–28

(2006) *Écrits*, trans. B. Fink. New York

Laird, A. (1993) "Sounding out ecphrasis: art and text in Catullus 64," *JRS* 83: 18–30

Laplanche, J. (1976) *Life and Death in Psychoanalysis*, trans. J. Mehlman. Baltimore

Leach, E. W. (1974) "Ekphrasis and the theme of artistic failure in Ovid's
*Metamorphoses*," *Ramus* 3: 102–42

(1997) "Venus, Thetis, and the social construction of maternal behavior," *CJ* 92:
347–71

Lee, M. O. (1996) *Virgil as Orpheus: A Study of the Georgics.* Albany

Liveley, G. (2003) "Tiresias/Teresa: a 'man-made-woman' in Ovid's *Metamorphoses*
3.318–38," *Helios* 30: 147–62

Loraux, N. (1998) *Mothers in Mourning*, trans. C. Pache. Ithaca

Lyne, R. O. A. M. (1987) *Further Voices in Vergil's* Aeneid. Oxford

(1989) *Words and the Poet: Characteristic Techniques of Style in Vergil's* Aeneid.
Oxford

Martin, C. (1992) *Catullus.* New Haven

Masson, J. M. (1985) *The Complete Letters of Sigmund Freud to Wilhelm Fliess,
1887–1904.* Cambridge, Mass.

Mathews, G. (2002) "*Non aliena tamen*: the erotics and poetics of narcissistic sado-
masochism in Propertius 1.15," *Helios* 29: 27–53

Mellard, J. M. (2006) *Beyond Lacan.* Albany

Miller, P. A. (2004) *Subjecting Verses: Latin Love Elegy and the Emergence of the Real.*
Princeton

Mitchell, J. (1982) "Introduction – I," in J. Mitchell and J. Rose (eds.) *Feminine
Sexuality.* New York, 1–26

Mitchell-Boyask, R. N. (1996) "*Sine fine*: Vergil's masterplot," *AJP* 117: 289–307

Morgan, L. (1999) *Patterns of Redemption in Vergil's* Georgics. Cambridge

Most, G. W. (1992) "*Disiecti membra poetae*: the rhetoric of dismemberment in
Neronian poetry," in R. Hexter and D. Selden (eds.) *Innovations of Antiquity.*
New York, 391–419

Newlands, C. E. (1995) *Playing With Time: Ovid and the* Fasti. Ithaca

Nugent, G. (1990) "This sex which is not one: de-constructing Ovid's hermaphrodite,"
*differences* 2: 160–85

(1992) "The voice of the women in *Aeneid* 5," *Arethusa* 25: 255–92

O'Gorman, E. (2004) "Cato the Elder and the destruction of Carthage," in Porter and
Buchan (2004b), 99–126

Oliensis, E. (2001) "Freud's *Aeneid*," *Vergilius* 47: 39–63

(2004) "Sibylline syllables: the intratextual *Aeneid*," *PCPS* 50: 29–45

(2009) "Psychoanalysis: Narcissus and Amphitruo," in A. Barchiesi and W. Scheidel (eds.) *The Oxford Handbook of Roman Studies*. Oxford

Orlando, F. (1978) *Toward a Freudian Theory of Literature*, trans. C. Lee. Baltimore

Panoussi, V. (2003) "*Ego maenas*: maenadism, marriage, and the construction of female identity in Catullus 63 and 64," *Helios* 30: 101–26

Porter, J. I. (2004) "Virgil's voids," in Porter and Buchan (2004b), 127–56

Porter, J. I. and Buchan, M. (2004a) "Introduction," in Porter and Buchan (2004b), 1–21

(eds.) (2004b) *Before Subjectivity? Lacan and the Classics = Helios* 31.1–2

Price, S. R. F. (1990) "The future of dreams: from Freud to Artemidorus," in D. M. Halperin, J. J. Winkler, and F. I. Zeitlin (eds.) *Before Sexuality: The Construction of Erotic Experience in the Ancient Greek World*. Princeton, 365–87

Putnam, M. C. J. (1982) *Essays on Latin Lyric, Elegy, and Epic*. Princeton

(1989) "Catullus 11 and Virgil *Aen.* 6.786–7," *Vergilius* 35: 28–30

(1993) "The languages of Horace *Odes* 1.24," *CJ* 88: 123–35

(1995) *Virgil's Aeneid: Interpretation and Influence*. Chapel Hill

Quinn, K. (1970) *Catullus: The Poems*. New York

(1972) *Catullus: An Interpretation*. London

Quint, D. (1993) *Epic and Empire*. Princeton

Ramsey, J. T. (2003) *Cicero: Philippics I–II*. Cambridge

Reckford, K. (1996) "Recognizing Venus (I)," *Arion* 3: 1–42

Ricciardi, A. (2003) *The Ends of Mourning: Psychoanalysis, Literature, Film*. Stanford

Richlin, A. (1999) "Cicero's head," in J. I. Porter (ed.) *Constructions of the Classical Body*. Ann Arbor, 190–211

Riffaterre, M. (1987) "The intertextual unconscious," in F. Meltzer (ed.) *The Trial(s) of Psychoanalysis*. Chicago, 211–25

Riviere, J. ([1929] 1986) "Womanliness as a masquerade," in V. Burgin, J. Donald, and C. Kaplan (eds.) *Formations of Fantasy*. London, 35–44

Rochette, B. (1997) "*Ruma* ou *roma?*," *Maia* 49: 215–17

Roller, L. E. (1999) *In Search of God the Mother: The Cult of Anatolian Cybele*. Berkeley

Sacks, P. M. (1985) *The English Elegy: Studies in the Genre from Spenser to Yeats*. Baltimore

Sandy, G. (1971) "Catullus 63 and the theme of marriage," *AJP* 92: 185–95

Sarkissian, J. (1983) *Catullus 68. An Interpretation*. Leiden

Schiesaro, A. (2003) *The Passions in Play: Thyestes and the Dynamics of Senecan Drama*. Cambridge

(2005) "Under the sign of Saturn: Dido's Kulturkampf," in J. P. Schwindt (ed.) *La représentation du temps dans la poésie augustéenne*. Heidelberg, 85–110

Schmale, M. (2004) *Bilderreigen und Erzähllabyrinth: Catulls Carmen 64*. Munich

Schmitz, T. A. (2007) *Modern Literary Theory and Ancient Texts: An Introduction*. Malden.

Segal, C. P. (1986) *Language and Desire in Seneca's Phaedra*. Princeton

(1994a) "Sophocles' *Oedipus Tyrannus*: Freud, language, and the unconscious," in P. L. Rudnytsky and E. H. Spitz (eds.) *Freud and Forbidden Knowledge*. New York, 72–95

(1994b) "Philomela's web and the pleasures of the text," in I. J. F. de Jong and J. P. Sullivan (eds.) *Modern Critical Theory and Classical Literature*. Leiden, 257–79

Segal, E. (1987) *Roman Laughter: The Comedy of Plautus*. 2nd edn. Oxford

Shaw, B. D. (2001) "Raising and killing children: two Roman myths," *Mnemosyne* 54: 31–77

Shoptaw, J. (2000) "Lyric cryptography," *Poetics Today* 21: 221–62

Skinner, M. B. (1997) "*Ego mulier*: the construction of male sexuality in Catullus," in J. P. Hallett and M. B. Skinner (eds.) *Roman Sexualities*. Princeton, 129–50

(2003) *Catullus in Verona*. Columbus

(2007a) "Authorial arrangement of the collection: debate past and present," in Skinner (2007b), 35–53

(ed.) (2007b) *A Companion to Catullus*. Malden

Slater, P. E. ([1968] 1992) *The Glory of Hera: Greek Mythology and the Greek Family*. Princeton

Sprengnether, M. (1990) *The Spectral Mother: Freud, Feminism, and Psychoanalysis*. Ithaca

Starobinski, J. (1987) "*Acheronta movebo*," in F. Meltzer (ed.) *The Trial(s) of Psychoanalysis*. Chicago, 273–86

Suzuki, M. (1989) *Metamorphoses of Helen: Authority, Difference, and the Epic*. Ithaca

Taylor, G. (2000) *Castration: An Abbreviated History of Western Manhood*. New York

Thibodeau, P. (2003) "Can Vergil cry? Epicureanism in Horace *Odes* 1.24," *CJ* 98: 243–56

Thomas, R. F. (1988) *Virgil: Georgics, vol. 2: Books III–IV*. Cambridge

Thomsen, O. (1992) *Ritual and Desire: Catullus 61 and 62 and Other Ancient Documents on Wedding and Marriage*. Aarhus

Thomson, D. F. S. (1997) *Catullus*. Toronto

Timpanaro, S. (1976) *The Freudian Slip: Psychoanalysis and Textual Criticism*, trans. K. Soper. London

Toohey, P. (2004) *Melancholy, Love, and Time: Boundaries of the Self in Ancient Literature*. Ann Arbor

Tsitsiou-Chelidoni, C. (2003) *Ovid Metamorphosen Buch VIII*. Frankfurt am Main

Vernant, J.-P. ([1967] 1988) "Oedipus without the complex," in *Tragedy and Myth in Ancient Greece*, trans. J. Lloyd. New York, 85–111

Weber, C. (2002) "The Dionysus in Aeneas," *CP* 97: 322–43

Wheeler, S. M. (1997) "Changing names: the miracle of Iphis in Ovid *Metamorphoses* 9," *Phoenix* 51: 190–202

Willbern, D. (1979) "Freud and the inter-penetration of dreams," *diacritics* 9: 98–110

Wiseman, T. P. (1984) "Cybele, Virgil and Augustus," in T. Woodman and D. West (eds.) *Poetry and Politics in the Age of Augustus*. Cambridge, 117–28

(1985) *Catullus and His World*. Cambridge

Wray, D. (2001) *Catullus and the Poetics of Manhood*. Cambridge

(2003) "What poets do: Tibullus on 'easy' hands," *CP* 98: 217–50

Wright, E. (1998) *Psychoanalytic Criticism: A Reappraisal*. 2nd edn. Cambridge

Young, E. M. (2008) "The mediated muse: Catullus and the poetics of lyric translation," unpublished dissertation, Berkeley

# Index of passages discussed

# General index